TABLE OF CONTENTS

2	INTRODUCTION
3	CHAKRAS: WHAT ARE THEY & WHY THEY'RE IMPORTANT
12	ROOT CHAKRA
16	SACRAL CHAKRA
20	SOLAR PLEXUS CHAKRA
27	HEART CHAKRA
33	THROAT CHAKRA
38	THIRD EYE CHAKRA
45	CROWN CHAKRA
54	GROUNDING HEALING POWERS REVEALED
59	ANIMAL'S HEALING POWERS & GROUNDING
65	TREES' MAGICAL HEALING BENEFITS
70	SOLAR FLARES & HEALING
77	BIOPLASMA CELL SALTS
89	CRYSTALS REVEALED
98	SELF-CARE {INEXPENSIVE BUT EFFECTIVE}
106	AURAS
120	FREQUENCY, WATER & HEALING
123	12TH DIMENSIONAL SHIELD
129	SPIRIT GUIDES
135	SYNCHRONICITIES
140	ANGEL NUMBERS
147	INTUITIVE ABILITIES - CLAIR'S
152	THE ASCENSION

Introduction

Welcome to a transformative journey of self-discovery, awakening, and ascension. This book is an invitation to explore the depths of your being and step into a higher state of consciousness. Within these pages, you will find a blend of personal anecdotes, profound insights, and practical guidance—tools to help you navigate the path of spiritual evolution.

Over decades, I've searched for the truth, and what you'll encounter here is a rich tapestry of wisdom designed to resonate with anyone on the quest for higher understanding. Whether you are just beginning your journey or have been on the path for some time, the insights offered within these pages are meant to support, challenge, and inspire you to reach beyond the limitations of the physical world and embrace the infinite potential of your true, divine essence.

As we venture through the sections you will discover how to unlock new levels of awareness, overcome obstacles, and embrace the process of ascension. This journey is about shedding the old and embracing the new, aligning with your highest self, and recognizing the divine within you and all around you. As an interactive tool, the **5D Navigator Journal** is available now to guide you further on your path.

I invite you to open your heart and mind as we embark on this adventure together. Let the wisdom in these pages guide you to a place of greater clarity, peace, and connection to your higher purpose.

QUICK MEDITATION: Protecting Your Energy Field

- Envision a sphere of white light surrounding you.
- Imagine a bright, protective sphere of white light enveloping your entire body. This light is warm, loving, and impenetrable, keeping you safe and shielded from any negativity.
- Affirm silently: "I am protected, surrounded by love, and open to divine guidance."

The Chakras

What They Are and Why They're Important?

The chakras are energy centers within the body that influence our physical, emotional, and spiritual well-being. The word "chakra" comes from the Sanskrit word for "wheel" or "disc," symbolizing spinning wheels of energy. There are seven main chakras aligned along the spine, each associated with different aspects of our life and connected to specific physical organs, emotions, and spiritual energies.

Healing Begins Within

Balancing these chakras is crucial for maintaining optimal health and harmony in our lives. When the chakras are open and aligned, energy flows freely through the body, leading to well-being and inner peace. However, when a chakra becomes blocked or unbalanced, it can result in physical discomfort, emotional struggles, or spiritual disconnection.

We will explore each of the seven main chakras, their significance, and how to keep them balanced.

Color Correction = Changes Cellular Memories

This book is frequency coded, and light coded. Why do think our Chakras have colors?

Finding Balance in Your Life

Your chakras are powerful energy centers that influence every part of your life. By taking the time to understand, balance, and heal them, you open yourself to a life filled with joy, health, and inner peace.

Remember: You have the power within you to create the life you want. Keep your energy flowing, stay true to yourself, and let your inner light shine!

Unlock Your Full Potential

Every chakra holds the potential to unlock a higher level of consciousness and self-awareness. By working on these energy centers, you tap into your own innate power. Whether it's the confidence and vitality of the Solar Plexus, the compassion of the Heart Chakra, or the wisdom of the Crown Chakra, each one allows you to access a greater version of yourself. You are capable of living a life full of purpose and fulfillment—chakra work can help you realize and embody that potential.

Small Steps Lead to Big Shifts

Chakra work doesn't have to be a huge, overwhelming task. Start with simple practices—whether it's a few minutes of mindful breathing, meditation, journaling, or using crystals or affirmations. These small, consistent efforts create lasting changes. As you progress, you'll notice subtle shifts in how you feel, think, and act, which will gradually lead to profound transformation. Every step counts.

The Power of Awareness

One of the most powerful tools you can use on your chakra journey is awareness. By bringing your attention to each chakra and tuning into how it feels physically, emotionally, and energetically, you unlock valuable insights into where you may need healing or attention. When you are aware, you can begin to make positive changes. Just by recognizing imbalances, you are already on your way to healing them.

Healing is a journey, not a Destination

There's no "perfect" state to achieve with your chakras—healing is an ongoing process. Some days may feel easier than others, and that's perfectly okay. Be gentle with yourself as you work through your energy centers. Trust that every effort you make is a step toward greater alignment, and honor yourself for the progress you're making, no matter how small it may seem.

Healing your chakras is an active process, and it involves personal commitment, consistent effort, and a willingness to confront and release the blockages in your energy.

A massive shift is occurring on Earth, with powerful waves of Light coming in as the veil of separation and denial lifts. These changes are affecting both the planet and our bodies. Earth is undergoing a transformation, and so are we. A process of transformation is taking place at the cellular level in our bodies.

Many people are waking up and remembering now because it was meant to happen at this time. Beings who have lived in dense physical bodies now have the option to exist in bodies of Light. This shift can feel jarring in some ways. You might experience strange physical vibrations that feel uncomfortable at times.

The changes happening in our bodies right now are activating the information stored in our DNA. Our DNA holds the most important blueprint of who we are, and it's now evolving. It will shift from two strands to twelve or even fourteen strands, which are linked to energy centers or chakras within and around us. This twelve-strand DNA was originally present in humans over 300,000 years ago.

This stepping up of energies is affecting every system in your body-nerves, muscles, vessels, skin, organs and glands as they try to adapt to the new frequencies.

You are the genetic engineers of the new world species. If you are willing, you must reorganize and rebuild your own DNA. You live in your body, and you will change it while you are in it. Some people have already started this process.

As energy beings, your chakras are keys to transforming your body.

The Guru's Role is to Empower, Not to "Fix" & "Control"

- A true guru or spiritual teacher is there to empower you by offering guidance, tools, and wisdom. They do not "fix" your chakras—they help you discover your own potential for healing and self-realization. You do not need or want a co-dependent relationship.

- They may teach you meditation techniques, breathwork, or practices that can help align your chakras, but you must implement these practices yourself. The guru's role is to guide you toward your own awakening.

- Why it matters: A guru or teacher can't make the changes for you. Their guidance helps you connect to your inner wisdom, but the work comes from your active participation. You may need to learn specific techniques or practices, but it's through your dedication that healing occurs.

- Each phase of your life may bring new challenges, and your chakras may need to be worked on again and again. Healing is an ongoing process, and the more you engage with your chakras, the more you learn about your own energy. No one else can walk this journey for you.

Chakra Work is Personal and Unique

Your chakras are deeply connected to your personal life experiences, emotions, beliefs, and energy. These energy centers are not just abstract concepts—they are reflections of your inner world. They represent your physical, emotional, mental, and spiritual health. No one else can fully know your inner landscape the way you do. While a guru can guide you and provide wisdom, the real transformation happens when you engage with your own energy.

Encouragement for Your Healing Journey

Chakra healing is not about seeking someone else to fix you—it's about discovering your own inner wisdom and power. A guru, teacher, or healer can be a guide, but the most important work is done by you. You have everything you need within you to balance, align, and heal your chakras. It may take time, effort, and patience, but every step you take toward understanding your energy is a step toward greater self-awareness, peace, and spiritual growth.

You are your own healer. Yes, you have the power to heal yourself! The more you engage with your chakras, the more you awaken to your limitless potential for transformation. Trust in your own abilities and know that every effort you make toward healing is a powerful act of self-love. The journey is yours, and you are more than capable of walking it.

Chakra alignment is a crucial aspect of overall well-being, as it directly influences your physical, emotional, mental, and spiritual health. When your chakras are aligned, your energy flows freely, bringing balance, clarity, and harmony into your life. Conversely, when your chakras are misaligned or blocked, you may experience imbalances in various areas, leading to physical ailments, emotional distress, or spiritual stagnation.

<u>Simple Chakra Clearing and Alignment Meditation</u>

- Take a few deep breaths. As you inhale, imagine you're breathing in calm, grounding energy from the earth. As you exhale, release any tension or stress.

- Visualize roots growing from the base of your spine, anchoring you to the earth. With each breath, feel more rooted and centered.

- Visualize a beautiful red rose blooming at the base of your spine. Picture its petals unfolding, and feel the sweet, earthy scent of the rose filling the air. As the flower opens, see a vibrant red light expanding, grounding you into the earth and making you feel safe and secure.

- Affirmation: "I am grounded. I am safe and supported."

- Take a moment to feel stable and rooted.

- Bring your awareness to your lower abdomen. Visualize an orange marigold blooming here. Imagine the petals opening wide and the scent of the marigold filling the air. See the color orange radiating from this flower, flowing through your body, and bringing warmth, creativity, and joy.

- Affirmation: "I am creative. I embrace joy and pleasure in my life."

- Feel your creativity and emotions flowing freely.

- Shift your focus to just above your navel. Visualize a radiant sunflower blooming here. Picture its bright yellow petals reaching toward the sky. The sunflower's scent fills you with energy, confidence, and vitality. As the flower opens, feel a surge of personal power and self-assurance.

- Affirmation: "*I am confident. I trust in my personal power.*"

- Let this yellow light fill you with warmth and strength.

- Bring your awareness to your heart. Visualize a gentle green lily blossoming here. The petals of the lily open slowly, releasing a fresh, uplifting scent of green. As the flower blooms, feel love, compassion, and healing energy flowing through your chest, softening your heart.

- Affirmation: "I am love. I am open to giving and receiving love."

- Shift your focus to your throat. Visualize a delicate bluebell flower blooming here. Imagine the cool blue petals gently opening and releasing a soothing scent. As the bluebell blooms, feel your throat opening and your ability to communicate clearly and authentically.

- Affirmation: "*I speak my truth with clarity and confidence.*"

- Allow your voice to feel free and unblocked.

- Bring your awareness to the space between your eyebrows. Visualize a calming lavender flower opening here. Its soft indigo petals release a soothing, calming fragrance. As the lavender blooms, feel your intuition growing stronger and your mind becoming clear and sharp.

- Affirmation: "*I trust my intuition. I am open to divine wisdom.*"

- Feel clarity and insight flowing through your mind.

- Finally, bring your awareness to the top of your head. Visualize a beautiful white lotus flower blooming here. Its petals open to reveal a brilliant light shining from within. The lotus releases a subtle, spiritual scent that connects you to higher consciousness and divine energy.

- Affirmation: "*I am connected to the divine. I am open to higher wisdom.*"

- Feel a sense of peace, unity, and spiritual connection.

- Now, see all seven flowers blooming and their colors blending together in harmony. Feel the energy of the flowers and their scents filling your entire being, aligning and balancing your chakras. The colors flow from your Root Chakra to your Crown Chakra, bringing perfect harmony to your body, mind, and spirit.

- Take a few deep breaths, feeling the alignment settle within you.

- Affirmation: "*I am whole. My chakras are balanced and aligned.*"

- When you're ready, gently bring your awareness back to the present moment. Wiggle your fingers and toes, and take a few deep, cleansing breaths.

- Open your eyes when you feel ready, bringing with you the sense of balance, peace, and alignment.

During the Spring and Summer, I love walking around my farm, allowing God and the Universe to guide me to the flowers. As I encounter each one, I absorb their colors and fragrances into my chakras, healing and recharging daily. It feels as though my spirit is drawn to exactly the flowers I need, providing the perfect energy for my healing.

Physical Health and Vitality

Chakras are linked to specific organs and bodily functions. Misaligned chakras can contribute to physical ailments. For example, blockages in the Throat Chakra (linked to the throat and communication) can lead to sore throats or difficulty expressing yourself. Alignment helps maintain optimal physical function, reduces the risk of illness, and enhances vitality.

WATER IS YOUR BEST FRIEND

Root Chakra (Muladhara)

Location: Base of your spine
Color: Red

- **Purpose**: Stability, safety, and grounding

- **Location**: Tailbone Area and is your foundation. When it's balanced, you feel grounded, secure, and confident in facing life's challenges. However, if it's blocked, you might feel anxious, insecure, or disconnected from your body.
    - Feeling fearful, anxious, or restless
    - Difficulty feeling "at home" anywhere
    - Financial stress or instability
    - May include lower back pain, constipation or fatigue

- **Physical Connection**: Legs, feet, bones, large intestine, adrenal glands

- **Ways to Balance**: Grounding exercises - walking barefoot on grass, yoga, meditation, and the use of red gemstones like garnet or red jasper.

How to unblock it:

- **Visualization**: Imagine a vibrant red light glowing at the base of your spine. As you breathe in, feel this light getting brighter, grounding you firmly to the earth.
- **Grounding exercises**: Walk barefoot on grass, soil, or sand. Reconnect with nature and feel the earth beneath you.
- **Affirmations**: *"I am safe. I am grounded. I belong here."*
- **Yoga poses**: Try poses like Mountain Pose or Tree Pose to establish balance and stability.

Top Foods to Balance and Energize the Root Chakra:

- **Root Vegetables** - Beets, carrots, sweet potatoes, radishes, parsnips, and turnips.
    - **Why They Help**: Root vegetables grow deep within the earth, making them naturally grounding and stabilizing. They provide essential vitamins, minerals, and fiber that support physical health.

- **Red Fruits and Vegetables** - Tomatoes, red bell peppers, strawberries, raspberries, pomegranates, cherries, cranberries, and red apples.
    - **Why They Help**: The red color is associated with the Root Chakra. These foods are rich in antioxidants, vitamin C, and nutrients that boost energy and support the immune system.

- **Protein-Rich Foods** - Eggs, red meat (grass-fed), beans, legumes, nuts, and seeds.
    - **Why They Help**: Protein is essential for building and repairing tissues, providing a sense of physical strength and stability. It helps keep you grounded and energized.

- **Whole Grains** - Brown rice, quinoa, oats, barley, and whole wheat.
    - **Why They Help**: Whole grains are rich in fiber and nutrients that stabilize blood sugar levels and provide long-lasting energy, promoting a sense of security and grounding.
- **Nuts and Seeds** - Almonds, walnuts, sunflower seeds, pumpkin seeds, chia seeds, and flaxseeds.
    - **Why They Help**: Nuts and seeds are grounding, rich in healthy fats, protein, and minerals like magnesium and zinc, which support overall health and vitality.
- **Spices and Herbs** - Ginger, garlic, cayenne pepper, paprika, and horseradish.
    - **Why They Help**: Spices can help stimulate the Root Chakra by warming the body, increasing circulation, and promoting a sense of energy and vitality.
- **Dark Leafy Greens** - Kale, spinach, collard greens, and Swiss chard.
    - **Why They Help**: While not red, leafy greens grow close to the earth and are rich in iron and other nutrients that support the blood, muscles, and overall physical health.
- **Healthy Fats** - Avocado, olive oil, coconut oil, and ghee.
    - **Why They Help**: Healthy fats are essential for grounding and nourishing the body, providing a steady source of energy and supporting brain function.

I have a huge garden every year. I provide all my neighbors and shut-ins with vegetables as well as all the animals that live here. Arugula begins growing here early Spring and is one of my favorites.

Crystals:

- **Red Jasper:** Grounding and stabilizing, provides a sense of safety and balance.
- **Hematite:** Helps to ground and connect you to the Earth's energy, fostering a sense of stability.
- **Smoky Quartz**: Clears negative energy, promotes calm, and strengthens your connection to the physical world.

How to use: Hold one of these crystals in your hand while meditating or place it on the base of your spine. Carry it in your pocket to feel grounded throughout the day.

See also: Crystal Chapter on how to clean and charge crystals.

Root Chakra Meditation

- Bring your awareness to the base of your spine. Visualize a spinning red light, like a vibrant ruby.
- Ask yourself: "Do I feel grounded, safe, and secure in my life right now?"
- If the energy feels dim or unsteady, visualize this red light growing brighter with each inhale. Imagine it spinning steadily and strongly.
- **Affirmation:** "I am safe, I am secure, I am grounded."

Sacral Chakra
(Svadhisthana)

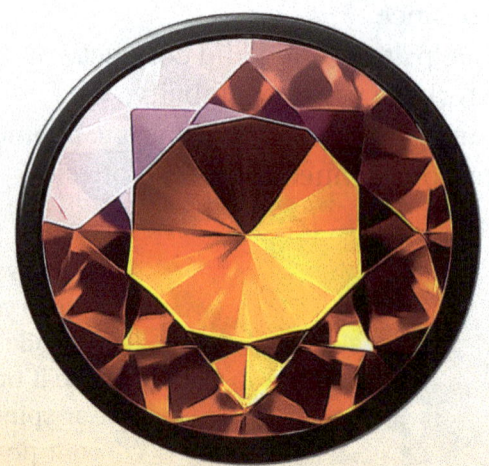

Location: Just below your belly button
Color: Orange

Purpose: Creativity, pleasure, and emotional well-being
Location: Lower Abdomen - just below your Naval Area. The Sacral Chakra governs your emotions, creativity, and passions.

- When it's open, you feel joyful, creative, and connected to your desires. A blocked sacral chakra can make you feel emotionally numb or creatively stuck.

Physical Connection: Reproductive organs, kidneys, bladder, circulatory system

Signs of imbalance:
- Lack of creativity or inspiration
- Feelings of guilt or shame
- Issues with intimacy and self-expression

How to unblock it:
- **Visualization:** Picture a warm, orange glow just below your navel, radiating outward. Feel its warmth as it flows through your body.
- **Creative activities:** Try painting, dancing, writing, or any activity that lets you express yourself. Consider starting a self-healing journal that you can write in daily as a reference guide. Draw pictures in it, be creative and make it a magical experience for yourself.
- **Water connection:** Spend time near water, whether it's a bath, a lake, or the ocean, to rejuvenate this chakra.

Top Foods to Nourish and Unblock the Sacral Chakra:

- **Orange Fruits and Vegetables** - Oranges, mandarins, carrots, pumpkins, sweet potatoes, butternut squash, and apricots.
  - **Why They Help:** The vibrant orange color of these foods is directly associated with the Sacral Chakra. They are rich in vitamins, especially vitamin C and beta-carotene, which boost vitality and stimulate creativity.

- **Hydrating Fruits** - Cantaloupe, watermelon, cucumber, coconut water, and peaches.
  - **Why They Help:** The Sacral Chakra is linked to the element of water. Consuming hydrating fruits helps to support fluidity and emotional balance, promoting better flow of energy in the body.

- **Nuts and Seeds** - Almonds, walnuts, cashews, pumpkin seeds, and sunflower seeds.
  - **Why They Help:** Nuts and seeds provide healthy fats and omega-3 fatty acids, which support hormone balance and enhance emotional stability. They also help with reproductive health, which is governed by the Sacral Chakra.
  - Pumpkin seeds are a natural dewormer

- **Healthy Fats** - Avocados, olives, olive oil, coconut oil, and flaxseed oil.
    - **Why They Help**: Healthy fats support hormone production and help nourish the body, promoting a sense of satisfaction and pleasure. They also aid in improving the function of the reproductive system.

- **Sweet and Warming Spices** - Cinnamon, nutmeg, ginger, cardamom, and clove.
    - **Why They Help**: Warming spices stimulate circulation, awaken the senses, and can enhance feelings of sensuality and creativity. They help improve digestion, which is often linked to Sacral Chakra imbalances.

- **Tropical Fruits** - Mangoes, papayas, pineapples, and passion fruits.
    - **Why They Help**: These fruits are juicy, sweet, and hydrating, which can help stimulate your senses and bring more joy and passion into your life.

- **Fermented Foods** - Sauerkraut, kimchi, yogurt, & kefir.
    - **Why They Help**: Fermented foods support a healthy gut microbiome, which is linked to emotional well-being. A balanced gut can improve your mood and help release emotional blockages.

- **Dark Chocolate (In Moderation)**
    - **Why It Helps**: Dark chocolate, especially if it's high in cocoa content, can enhance feelings of pleasure and stimulate the release of endorphins, supporting the Sacral Chakra's focus on joy and pleasure.

Crystals:
- **Carnelian**: Enhances creativity, confidence, and motivation, while also boosting joy and passion.
- **Orange Calcite:** Removes blockages and revitalizes your energy, especially for creative endeavors.
- **Sunstone**: Brings warmth, joy, and a sense of playfulness, helping you embrace life's pleasures.
- Carry or meditate with crystals like Carnelian, Orange Calcite, or Moonstone to balance and energize the Sacral Chakra. These are just a few of the orange crystals.

How to use: Place the crystal just below your navel during meditation or keep it nearby when working on creative projects.

See Chapter on Crystal cleaning and charging prior to healing with crystals.

Sacral Chakra Meditation:

Move your focus to your lower abdomen, just below your belly button. Picture a warm, glowing orange light.

- Ask yourself: "*Am I embracing joy, creativity, and pleasure in my life?*"
- If it feels blocked or dull, imagine the orange light growing brighter and more vibrant, expanding in warmth with each breath.
- Affirmation: "*I am creative, joyful, and open to the flow of life.*"

Solar Plexus Chakra (Manipura)

Location: Above your belly button
Color: Yellow

Purpose: The Solar Plexus Chakra is your center of personal power and confidence. When balanced, you feel empowered, motivated, and in control of your life.
- **Element**: Fire
- **Associated with**: Personal power, confidence, willpower, and self-esteem.

Physical Connection: Digestive system, liver, pancreas, stomach.

Signs of Imbalance: Low self-esteem, lack of direction, indecisiveness, or feeling powerless. Physical symptoms may include digestive issues, stomach ulcers, or fatigue.
- A blocked solar plexus can lead to feelings of self-doubt, low motivation, or a lack of direction.

Ways to Balance: Practicing affirmations, breathwork, sunlight exposure, and using yellow gemstones like citrine or tiger's eye.

To help clear and balance this chakra - it's essential to eat foods that resonate with its yellow color and support the element of fire, which represents transformation and energy.

Top Foods to Nourish and Unblock the Solar Plexus Chakra
- **Yellow Fruits and Vegetables** - Lemons, bananas, pineapples, yellow bell peppers, corn, and yellow squash.
  - **Why They Help**: Yellow foods correspond to the color of the Solar Plexus Chakra, helping to stimulate and energize it. These foods are rich in vitamins, especially vitamin C, which boosts your immune system and supports energy levels.

- **Whole Grains and Complex Carbohydrates** -Brown rice, quinoa, oats, barley, and millet.
  - **Why They Help**: Whole grains provide slow-releasing energy, supporting the Solar Plexus Chakra's focus on vitality and personal power. They also promote digestive health, which is closely linked to this chakra.

- **Spices for Warming and Activation** - Ginger, turmeric, cinnamon, cayenne pepper, and cumin.
  - **Why They Help**: The Solar Plexus Chakra is associated with the fire element. Warming spices can help stimulate digestion, increase metabolism, and boost your inner fire.

- **Legumes and Beans** - Lentils, chickpeas, black beans, and mung beans.
  - **Why They Help**: Legumes are packed with fiber and protein, which help stabilize blood sugar levels, support digestion, and provide sustained energy—perfect for maintaining a balanced Solar Plexus Chakra.

- **Nuts and Seeds** - Sunflower seeds, flaxseeds, pumpkin seeds, almonds, and cashews.
    - **Why They Help**: Nuts and seeds are rich in healthy fats, protein, and essential nutrients that support the body's energy production and help boost confidence and personal power.

- **Fermented Foods for Digestive Health** - Sauerkraut, kimchi, yogurt, kefir, and miso.
    - **Why They Help**: The Solar Plexus Chakra is closely linked to the digestive system. Fermented foods support gut health, which can improve mood, energy levels, and overall confidence.

- **Protein-Rich Foods** - Lean meats, eggs, tofu, and fish.
    - **Why They Help**: Protein is essential for building and repairing tissues, increasing stamina, and boosting your energy levels, which is vital for the Solar Plexus Chakra.

- **Healthy Fats for Sustained Energy** - Avocados, olive oil, ghee, and coconut oil.
    - **Why They Help**: Healthy fats provide a steady source of energy, supporting both the digestive system and the metabolism, which are governed by the Solar Plexus Chakra.

- **Herbal Teas to Support the Solar Plexus Chakra**
    - **Chamomile Tea:** Soothes the digestive system and reduce stress.
    - **Ginger Tea**: Aids digestion, boosts metabolism, and stimulates inner warmth.
    - **Peppermint Tea:** Eases digestive discomfort and promotes a sense of calm.

During the Summer, I always cut fresh flowers and place them in the house. Zinnias and Cosmos are beautiful, easy to grow and I save the seeds for the following year.

How to unblock it:
- **Visualization:** Imagine a bright, golden sun glowing in your solar plexus area. As you inhale, feel its warmth energizing you.
- **Core exercises:** Strengthen your core with yoga poses like Boat Pose or Plank.
- **Affirmations:** "*I am confident. I trust my abilities. I am in control of my life.*"
- **Breathwork:** Practice deep, diaphragmatic breathing to energize your center.

Clearing and balancing the solar plexus chakra (Manipura) is essential for self-confidence, personal power, and motivation.

Crystals that can help clear and balance the solar plexus chakra:

1. Citrine
- **Properties:** Known as the "stone of abundance" and personal power, citrine enhances confidence, motivation, and self-esteem.
  - It also helps to clear out negative energy and promote a positive outlook.
  - Carry a citrine stone in your pocket or place it on your solar plexus area during meditation.

Refer to chapter on Crystal cleaning and charging techniques.

2. **Yellow Jasper**
  - **Properties:** This grounding stone helps boost energy, protect your aura, and build confidence.

  - It is known for helping you stay focused and determined in achieving your goals.
  - How to Use: Hold yellow jasper during meditation to enhance your willpower and clarity.

3. **Tiger's Eye**
  - **Properties:** A powerful stone for courage and strength, tiger's eye is excellent for increasing confidence and promoting self-discipline. It helps balance emotions and brings clarity to decision-making.

  - Wear tiger's eye as a bracelet or place it on your solar plexus while meditating to boost personal power.

4. **Pyrite**
  - **Properties:** Often called "fool's gold," pyrite is known for its protective and energizing properties. It supports confidence, mental clarity, and the drive to take action.

  - Place pyrite on your desk or workspace to boost motivation or carry it with you to enhance your inner strength.

5. Amber
- **Properties:** Amber is fossilized tree resin that carries warm, solar energy. It helps to clear negative energy, release fears, and promote a sense of calm confidence.

  - Wear amber jewelry or place a piece on your solar plexus during meditation to clear energy blockages.

6. Sunstone
- **Properties:** Sunstone is known for bringing joy, enthusiasm, and optimism. It helps you feel empowered to shine your light and express your authentic self.

  - Meditate with sunstone on your solar plexus or wear it as a pendant to enhance your inner glow and vitality.

Yellow Colored Crystals

There are many other crystals that will help balance your Solar Plexus Chakra. When you select your crystal, you will have a "knowing" it will call out to you. Crystals are living, ancient beings just waiting for you to find them. They come into your light at the perfect time. Take what resonates with you and use it.

By using these crystals regularly, you can help clear blockages in your solar plexus chakra, increasing your confidence, motivation, and inner strength.

If you're having trouble deciding between 2 or more crystals, you can make a Crystal Grid with them.

Chakra Grid: Create a crystal grid using a combination of these stones. Place the grid in a space where you spend a lot of time to continuously clear and energize your solar plexus chakra.

Solar Plexus Chakra Meditation

- Shift your attention to the area above your belly button. Visualize a bright yellow sun shining in your solar plexus.

- Ask yourself: "*Do I feel confident and in control of my life?*"

- If this area feels weak or closed off, imagine the yellow light growing brighter, like a sun that fills your entire abdomen with warmth and strength.

- **Affirmations with Crystals**: Hold your chosen crystal and repeat affirmations like:
    - "*I am confident and empowered.*"
    - "*I trust myself to make the right decisions.*"
    - "*My personal power is strong, steady, and radiant.*"

- After doing this, drop your crystal in your pocket as a reminder throughout your day what your affirmations were! It never hurts having some moral support with you.

Heart Chakra
(Anahata)

Location: Center of your chest
Color: Green

Purpose: Love, compassion, and relationships.
Location: The Heart Chakra is the **bridge** between your lower chakras (related to the physical world) and your upper chakras (related to the spiritual).

Physical Connection: Heart, lungs, respiratory, cardiovascular, thymus gland, immune system, upper back, shoulders and chest area, arms, hands and touch.

Healthy/Open Heart Chakra: When it's open, you feel love, empathy, and compassion for yourself and others. A blocked heart chakra can result in feeling isolated or unable to connect with others.

Signs of imbalance:
- Difficulty trusting or opening up to others.
- Holding onto grudges or resentment.
- Feeling disconnected from loved ones.
- Heart-related issues: palpitations, chest pain, or irregular heartbeat.
- Lung problems: asthma, bronchitis, or other respiratory issues.
- Weak immune system: frequent colds or infections.
- Muscle tension in the upper back, shoulders, or chest.
- Poor circulation in the arms and hands.
- Chronic fatigue or low energy levels.

The heart chakra is linked to the color green, so naturally, green foods are especially powerful for clearing and energizing this chakra. Additionally, foods that promote overall cardiovascular health and emotional well-being can support the heart chakra.

Top Foods to Unblock and Balance the Heart Chakra

1. Leafy Greens
- Spinach, kale, Swiss chard, collard greens, and arugula are rich in nutrients and chlorophyll, which helps cleanse the body and support heart health.
- These greens boost circulation, reduce inflammation, and nourish the heart chakra.

2. Green Vegetables
- Broccoli, zucchini, green beans, celery, and cucumbers are alkalizing and help clear blockages in the heart chakra.
- These vegetables are high in antioxidants and vitamins that support heart function.
- Aloe Vera Plants in your house clean your air and are great companions in case you get burned. They require little water and love the sunlight. I have a large one in my kitchen. I call her TOPO.

3. Avocados
- Avocados are rich in healthy fats, which promote cardiovascular health and improve blood flow. I eat them raw and squeeze fresh lime juice over them.
- They also contain potassium and magnesium, which help relax the heart and support emotional balance.

4. Green Fruits
- Kiwi, green apples, grapes, and pears are hydrating and rich in nutrients that help clear and balance the heart chakra.
- These fruits are high in vitamin C, which is beneficial for both the physical heart and emotional well-being.

5. Cruciferous Vegetables
- Brussels sprouts, cabbage, and bok choy are excellent for detoxifying the body and supporting the immune system.
- They help cleanse the body of toxins that may be energetically blocking the heart chakra.

6. Herbs & Spices
- Basil, thyme, rosemary, and sage are heart-healthy herbs that can enhance circulation and reduce inflammation.
- Hawthorn berries are especially known for supporting heart health and opening the heart chakra.
- Cayenne pepper improves blood flow and stimulates energy throughout the body, which can help clear blockages.

7. Nuts and Seeds
- Almonds, walnuts, flaxseeds, and chia seeds are high in healthy fats, which support the cardiovascular system and promote emotional stability.
- These foods are also rich in magnesium, which helps relax the heart muscles.

8. Green Tea
- Green tea is packed with antioxidants that promote heart health and calm the mind.
- It helps increase feelings of compassion and relaxation, which are connected to a balanced heart chakra.

9. Dark Chocolate (in moderation)
- High-quality dark chocolate with a high cocoa content (70% or more) is rich in antioxidants and helps release endorphins, which can uplift your mood and promote love.
- It can also support heart health by improving blood flow.

10. Watermelon
- Though not green, watermelon is great for the heart chakra as it hydrates the body and contains lycopene, which supports heart health.
- It's refreshing nature can help clear emotional blockages and open you up to love.

By incorporating these foods into your diet, you can help unblock the heart chakra, allowing for greater love, compassion, and emotional healing.

Heart Chakra-Balancing Recipe Idea

Green Smoothie: Blend spinach, avocado, kiwi, cucumber, green apple, a handful of parsley, and a splash of coconut water.

Unblocking the heart chakra (Anahata) is essential for cultivating love, compassion, forgiveness, and emotional balance. Here are some crystals that are particularly effective for clearing and balancing the heart chakra:

1. Rose Quartz
- **Properties:** Known as the "stone of unconditional love," it opens the heart chakra to self-love, compassion, and healing. Rose quartz promotes emotional healing and helps release past wounds.

- Place it on your chest during meditation or keep it by your bedside to attract loving energy.

2. Green Aventurine
- **Properties:** This is a stone of optimism and emotional healing. It brings harmony and calm, helping you release old emotional patterns and open your heart to new experiences.

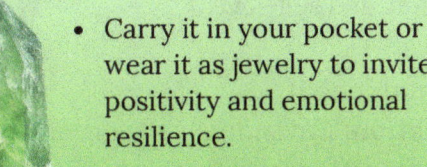

- Carry it in your pocket or wear it as jewelry to invite positivity and emotional resilience.

There are many other heart chakra crystals waiting for you to find them. Examples are: Rhodonite, green jade, Malachite, Amazonite, Pink Tourmaline, Emerald, Prehnite, and Chrysoprase. In my experience, finding them is half the fun.

How to Use Crystals to Unblock the Heart Chakra
- **Crystal Meditation:** Lie down and place your chosen crystal on your heart chakra (center of your chest). Focus on your breath and visualize green or pink light expanding from the crystal, filling your heart space.
- **Crystal Grids:** Create a crystal grid using a combination of heart chakra stones (like rose quartz, green aventurine, and rhodonite) to amplify healing energy.
- **Wearing Crystals:** Wear a necklace or bracelet with your chosen heart chakra crystal to keep its energy close to your heart throughout the day.
- **Bath Ritual:** Add a few tumbled stones (like rose quartz or green aventurine) to a warm bath to infuse the water with loving, healing energy. Be sure to only use water-safe crystals.

Affirmations with Crystals: Hold your chosen crystal while repeating affirmations such as:
- *"I am open to giving and receiving love."*
- *"My heart is open, balanced, and full of light."*
- *"I forgive myself and others, and I release all past hurts."*

By incorporating these crystals into your daily practice, you can help clear blockages in your heart chakra, fostering emotional healing, compassion, and self-love.

How to unblock it
Visualization: Envision a soft, green light expanding from your heart, enveloping your entire body.
- **Heart-opening exercises**: Practice yoga poses like Cobra Pose or Camel Pose.
- **Affirmations:** "*I am open to love. I forgive myself and others. I am connected.*"
- **Gratitude practice**: Write down three things you are grateful for each day. Seriously consider starting a journal. I'm grateful I did because I use it for accountability and inspiration when I need it to stay the path.

Throat Chakra (Vishuddha)

Location: Throat area
Color: Blue
Element: Ether (Space)

Purpose: Throat Chakra governs your communication, self-expression, truth, and authenticity. It governs your ability to speak your truth and express yourself clearly. A balanced Throat Chakra allows for honest communication and authentic self-expression.

Location: Throat

Physical Connection: Throat, vocal cords, mouth, thyroid gland.

Signs of Imbalance: Fear of speaking up, difficulty in expressing thoughts, or feeling misunderstood. Physical symptoms may include sore throats, thyroid issues, or neck pain.

Ways to Balance Your Throat Chakra

1. Affirmations & Self-Talk
- Use affirmations to reinforce your intention of unblocking your throat chakra:
    - "I speak my truth with confidence."
    - "My voice matters, and I am heard."
    - "I express myself freely and openly."

- Practice positive self-talk, especially if you struggle with self-doubt or fear of speaking up.

2. Breathwork & Deep Breathing
- Ujjayi Pranayama (Ocean Breath): Inhale deeply through your nose, then exhale slowly, slightly contracting the back of your throat to create a soft ocean-like sound. This technique helps to clear blockages and calm your mind.
- Simply practicing slow, deep breaths can also help clear energy blockages in the throat.

3. Sound Healing
- Humming, chanting, or singing can stimulate the throat chakra. Try chanting the mantra "HAM" (the sound associated with the throat chakra) during meditation.
- Listening to healing frequencies like 741 Hz can also help balance the throat chakra.

4. Essential Oils & Aromatherapy
- Diffuse or apply oils like peppermint, eucalyptus, lavender, or frankincense on your throat area to stimulate and open the chakra.

I grow lavender all around my farm so I have fresh. I dry it for the cold months and use it regularly.

5. **Crystals for Throat Chakra**
   - **Wear or meditate with crystals. Some examples are:**
     - **Blue lace agate**: Calms and encourages clear communication.
     - **Aquamarine**: Helps you express your emotions and speak your truth.
     - **Lapis lazuli**: Enhances self-expression and inner truth.
   - Place a crystal on your throat area during meditation or simply carry it with you throughout the day.

Lapis usually stays on my nightstand or under my pillow.

Refer to chapter on Crystals cleaning and charging prior to using any for healing.

6. **Yoga Poses for the Throat Chakra**
   - Fish Pose (Matsyasana): Opens up the throat and chest.
   - Shoulder Stand (Sarvangasana): Stimulates the throat chakra and enhances blood flow.
   - Cat-Cow Pose (Marjaryasana-Bitilasana): Moves energy through the throat area while increasing flexibility in your spine.
   - Lion's Breath: Kneel, take a deep breath, open your mouth wide, stick out your tongue, and exhale forcefully, making a "ha" sound. This clears tension from the throat.

7. Practice Active Listening & Honest Communication
- Be mindful of your words and intentions in conversations.
- Speak your truth but also be a good listener. When you actively listen, you create a balanced flow of communication, which is essential for a healthy throat chakra.

8. Journal or Write
- Writing down your thoughts, feelings, and fears can release blocked energy. You can also try stream-of-consciousness writing where you write without censoring yourself.

9. Diet & Hydration
- Drink plenty of water to keep the throat hydrated.
- Incorporate blue foods like blueberries, blackberries, and herbal teas like chamomile or peppermint.

10. Massage & Physical Touch
- Gently massage your neck and throat area to release tension.

Incorporate a few of these practices consistently, and you'll likely notice an improvement in your ability to communicate clearly, express yourself authentically, and feel more aligned with your inner truth. Remember your inner truth will not always align with others' inner truth.

Top Foods to Support a Healthy Throat Chakra

- **Blue-Colored Foods** - Since the throat chakra is linked to the color blue, incorporating naturally blue foods can help balance its energy. Some examples are Blueberries, Blackberries, Blue grapes, and Elderberries.
- I enjoy picking fresh black raspberries on my farm when I'm mowing the other side of the River.

- The throat chakra is associated with **fluidity and the element of ether**. Hydrating the body supports the flow of energy in this chakra.

    - Water (infused with lemon or cucumber)
    - Avoid CITY Water because of FLOURIDE
    - Coconut water
    - Herbal teas such as:
        - Peppermint (cooling and soothing for the throat)
        - Chamomile (calming and anti-inflammatory)
        - Licorice root (supports throat health)
        - Lemongrass (cleansing and refreshing)

Use what intuitively resonates with you and discard the rest. Everyone is on an individual ascension path and what may work for you may not work for someone else.

THROAT CHAKRA MEDITATION:

- Focus on your throat area.
- Picture a clear blue light, like a shimmering blue ocean.
- Ask yourself: "*Am I able to express my truth clearly and confidently?*"
- If this chakra feels constricted, visualize the blue light expanding, clearing away any blockages. Allow your throat to relax and open.
- Affirmation: "*I speak my truth with clarity and kindness.*"

You can also tap on the throat chakra area while saying positive affirmations to release energy blockages.

Third Eye Chakra
(Ajna)

Location: Between your eyebrows
Color: Indigo

Purpose: Intuition, wisdom, and insight
Location: Between the eyebrows, slightly above the bridge of the nose
- The Third Eye Chakra helps you see beyond the surface, connecting you to your intuition and inner wisdom.
- It is associated with intuition, perception, wisdom, and a deeper understanding of both the seen and unseen realms.

Element: Light (or Ether)
Sense: Extra-sensory perception (ESP)
Physical Connection: Pineal gland

The third eye chakra is believed to be the seat of intuition, insight, and higher consciousness. It governs your ability to see beyond the physical world, allowing you to perceive deeper truths, understand patterns, and connect with your inner wisdom.

Functions of the Third Eye Chakra
- **Intuition & Psychic Abilities:** The third eye is often linked to psychic abilities such as clairvoyance (clear seeing), clairaudience (clear hearing), and claircognizance (clear knowing).
- **Imagination & Creativity**: It helps you visualize, imagine new possibilities, and access creative inspiration.
- **Perception & Insight:** The third eye is connected to the ability to see things clearly, both literally and metaphorically. It helps with self-awareness, self-reflection, and seeing the bigger picture in life.
- **Spiritual Awareness:** It serves as a gateway to higher consciousness and spiritual realms, aiding in meditation, spiritual growth, and mystical experiences.
- **Mental Clarity & Focus**: A balanced third eye chakra can help you concentrate, make better decisions, and solve problems with clarity.

Purpose: Intuition, wisdom, and insight

Location: The Third Eye Chakra helps you see beyond the surface, connecting you to your intuition and inner wisdom. When it's open, you trust your inner guidance.
- A blocked third eye can cause confusion or lack of clarity.
- Signs of imbalance:
- Difficulty trusting your intuition
- Feeling lost or indecisive
- Headaches or eye strain

Here are some foods and practices that can help balance and activate this chakra:

1. Foods that are dark, purple, and indigo colored.
- **Blueberries**: Rich in antioxidants that support brain health.
- **Blackberries**: Aid in detoxification and boost mental clarity.
- **Purple grapes**: Full of phytonutrients that enhance focus.
- **Plums and prunes**: Support a healthy digestive system, which is linked to mental clarity.
- **Eggplant**: Provides antioxidants and nutrients that support brain function.
- **Red cabbage**: Contains anthocyanins that promote neurological health.

2. Nutrient-Rich Vegetables - these vegetables enhance mental clarity and intuition:

- **Beets:** Improve blood flow to the brain, aiding in spiritual awareness. Antioxidants: Beets contain antioxidants like lutein and zeaxanthin, which are known to support eye health and protect against oxidative stress. Beets are high in nitrates, which your body converts into nitric oxide. Nitric oxide helps improve blood flow and oxygen delivery to the brain, enhancing cognitive function and clarity.

I never used to like beets, so I began with adding the leaves to my salads. Then I tried homemade pickled beets in vinegar and oil. Now, I grow them yearly in my garden.

- **Carrots**: High in beta-carotene, promoting eye health and vision (symbolically linked to the "third eye").
- **Spinach and kale**: Rich in vitamins and minerals that support brain function.

3. Healthy Fats - The brain is composed largely of fat, and healthy fats are essential for brain health:

- **Avocados**: Provides healthy fats that improve brain function.

Avocados took me years to acquire the taste for. Then I was told to squeeze lime juice over them and I love them now.

- **Walnuts**: Contain omega-3 fatty acids, which support mental clarity and reduce brain fog.
- **Coconut oil**: Known to boost cognitive function and enhance spiritual awareness.
- **Chia seeds and flaxseeds**: Provide omega-3 fatty acids that enhance mental clarity.

4. Herbs and Spices - certain herbs can stimulate the third eye and improve spiritual awareness:

- **Turmeric**: Known for its anti-inflammatory properties, it enhances brain function and spiritual clarity.
- **Ginger**: Boosts circulation and opens up energy channels.
- **Gotu kola**: A traditional herb for enhancing memory and intuition.
- **Ginkgo biloba**: Improves circulation to the brain and supports mental clarity.
- **Lavender and rosemary**: Both are known to calm the mind, allowing for deeper intuition.

5. Detoxifying Teas - Herbal teas that support the third eye:
- **Mugwort tea**: Used traditionally to enhance dreams and spiritual visions.
- **Green tea**: Contains L-theanine, which improves focus and relaxation.
- **Chaga mushroom tea**: Known for its antioxidant properties that support brain health.

6. Raw Cacao -
- **Dark chocolate (70%+ cacao)**: The flavonoids in dark chocolate improve blood flow by stimulating the production of nitric oxide, which relaxes blood vessels. Dark chocolate is rich in antioxidants like polyphenols, which help neutralize harmful free radicals in the body. Dark chocolate contains compounds like theobromine and phenylethylamine, which can help reduce stress and promote relaxation.

7. Hydration -
- **Water**: Staying hydrated is essential for mental clarity and spiritual openness.
- **Lemon water**: Helps detoxify the body and improve focus.
- **Cucumber water**: Cucumbers are rich in antioxidants like vitamin C and beta-carotene, which help combat oxidative stress and support overall health. Cucumbers provide potassium, which helps balance electrolytes and supports kidney function in filtering out toxins.
- **Coconut water**: Provides electrolytes that support energy flow in the body.

8. Pineal Gland Detox Foods - the pineal gland is often associated with the third eye chakra. To detoxify it:
- **Chlorella and spirulina**: Remove heavy metals that can calcify the pineal gland.
- **Cilantro**: Cilantro helps remove toxic heavy metals like lead, mercury, and aluminum from your tissues. It binds to these metals, loosening them from your body and aiding in their elimination
- **Apple cider vinegar**: Helps decalcify the pineal gland.

Unblocking your third eye chakra (Ajna) involves a combination of physical, mental, and spiritual practices. The third eye is connected to intuition, inner vision, and spiritual insight. If you feel your intuition is clouded, or you're struggling to connect to your inner wisdom, consider these effective ways to activate and unblock your third eye chakra:

1. Meditation: Focus on the Third Eye: Sit in a quiet place, close your eyes, and direct your awareness to the spot between your eyebrows. Visualize a deep indigo light glowing in this area. Imagine it becoming brighter as you breathe in deeply.

- **Mantra Chanting**: The sound "OM" (AUM) is associated with the third eye chakra. Chanting this mantra can help activate the chakra and clear energy blockages.

2. Sun Gazing: Morning or Evening: Spend a few minutes looking at the rising or setting sun (never during midday). This practice is believed to stimulate the pineal gland (often associated with the third eye) and enhance spiritual awareness.

- Note: *To safely practice sungazing, only gaze at the sun during the first hour after sunrise or the last hour before sunset, starting with a few seconds and gradually increasing the time. Always listen to your body and stop immediately if you feel discomfort to protect your eyes.*

3. Breathwork (Pranayama):
- **Alternate Nostril Breathing (Nadi Shodhana)**: This breathing technique balances both hemispheres of the brain, promoting mental clarity and spiritual connection.
- **Kapalabhati (Breath of Fire)**: This energizing breath technique helps clear energy channels, promoting a clear mind.

4. Crystals and Gemstones: Amethyst, Lapis Lazuli, and Sodalite: These stones resonate with the third eye chakra. Place them on your forehead during meditation or carry them throughout the day.

- **Fluorite**: Known for enhancing spiritual insight, fluorite can be placed near your bed or in meditation spaces.

5. **Essential Oils and Aromatherapy:**
   - **Frankincense, Sandalwood, and Clary Sage**: These oils can stimulate the third eye. You can diffuse them, apply diluted drops to your forehead, or add them to your bath.
   - **Lavender**: Calming and relaxing, it helps open the mind to intuition.

6. **Diet and Nutrition: Detoxify the Pineal Gland:**
   - The pineal gland is often associated with the third eye. Foods like chlorella, spirulina, raw cacao, and cilantro help detoxify it.
   - Consume Dark, Purple Foods: Blueberries, blackberries, and purple grapes align with the indigo frequency of the third eye chakra.

7. **Sound Healing**: Binaural Beats and Solfeggio Frequencies:
   - Listening to 963 Hz or 432 Hz frequencies can help activate the third eye chakra.
   - Tibetan Singing Bowls: Use them during meditation to create vibrations that resonate with the third eye. (Research Youtube for examples).

8. **Yoga Asanas: Forward Bends and Inversions:**
   - Poses like Child's Pose (Balasana), Downward-Facing Dog (Adho Mukha Svanasana), and Shoulder Stand (Sarvangasana) increase blood flow to the head, stimulating the third eye chakra.
   - Eagle Pose (Garudasana): Helps focus energy and brings awareness to the forehead area.

9. **Visualization and Creative Practices:**
   - **Third Eye Visualization**: Imagine an indigo lotus or light at your third eye while meditating.
   - **Journaling**: Write down your dreams, intuitions, or visions. This helps you become more aware of your inner guidance.

10. **Detox Your Lifestyle:**
    - **Limit Fluoride**: fluoride can calcify the pineal gland. Consider using fluoride-free toothpaste and drinking purified water.
    - **Reduce Processed Foods and Sugar**: These can dull your intuition. Focus on a clean, plant-based diet for clarity.

11. **Practice Mindfulness and Inner Reflection:** Spend Time in Nature:
    - Disconnect from technology and immerse yourself in nature to clear your mind and connect to your inner self.
    - Mindful Observation: Practice observing your thoughts without judgment. This helps you develop a deeper connection to your intuition.

12. **Affirmations for the Third Eye Chakra:**
    - *"I trust my intuition and inner guidance."*
    - *"I am open to the wisdom of the universe."*
    - *"I see clearly with my inner vision."*

13. **Lucid Dreaming and Dream Journaling**
    - Before bed, set the intention to remember your dreams.
    - Keep a journal by your bedside and write down any symbols or insights you receive upon waking.

Note: I sleep with crystals under my pillow. Some of my third eye favorites are laborite and lapis. Additionally, I keep orgonites either around my living space or in my pocket. Earth Family Crystals is a good source for the pocket orgonites.

Orgonite is a substance made by mixing organic materials (like resin) with inorganic ones (like metal shavings and quartz crystals). It was created by Dr. Wilhelm Reich to balance and harmonize energy by absorbing negative energy from the environment and transforming it into positive energy. People use orgonite for various benefits, such as EMF protection, energy balancing, environmental purification, improved sleep and relaxation, and supporting spiritual practices. The crystals inside react and harness the energy creating a piezoelectric effect sucking in the negative energy and transmutes into pure non-chaotic energy. Yes, the type of crystals inside determines the transmutation.

Crown Chakra
(Sahasrara)

Location: Top of your head
Color: Violet or white

Purpose: Spiritual connection and enlightenment. The Crown Chakra connects you to your higher self and the universe.

- When it's open, you feel a deep sense of peace and oneness. A blocked crown chakra can make you feel disconnected or spiritually lost.

Physical Connection: The Crown Chakra is located at the very top of the head, often referred to as the "crown" of the body. Some also describe it as being above the head, in the aura.

Element: The element associated with the Crown Chakra is thought or cosmic energy. It's the realm beyond the physical, associated with the formless, the transcendent, and the infinite.

Crown Chakra Purpose

- **Spirituality:** The Crown Chakra is closely linked to higher states of awareness, the divine, and universal consciousness. It's where we connect to our higher self and to the collective consciousness of humanity.

- **Enlightenment:** This chakra is considered the gateway to spiritual enlightenment and awakening. It governs the ability to experience profound peace, understanding, and connection to the divine.

- **Universal Oneness:** It embodies the concept of unity with the universe and transcending individuality. When this chakra is balanced, you feel a deep sense of interconnection with all living things.

- **Intuition & Wisdom:** It's the center of wisdom, intuition, and divine understanding. It encourages openness to receiving insights from higher realms of existence.

- **Faith and Trust:** When the Crown Chakra is balanced, individuals tend to have strong faith in their path and trust in the universe, knowing that they are part of something larger than themselves.

Signs of a Balanced Crown Chakra

- A deep sense of inner peace and connection to the universe.
- Clarity of mind and higher wisdom.
- A sense of unity and oneness with others and the world.
- Spiritual awakening or a profound understanding of the meaning of life.
- Feelings of bliss, transcendence, and calmness.

Signs of an Imbalanced Crown Chakra

- **Overactive**: A person may become overly focused on spiritual matters, losing touch with the practical aspects of life. They might also experience confusion, a lack of groundedness, or disconnection from reality.

- **Underactive**: A person may feel spiritually disconnected, lack a sense of purpose or direction, feel isolated, or struggle with depression and despair. There may be a sense of spiritual stagnation or lack of meaning in life.

- **Symptoms of imbalance** may also include mental fog, confusion, lack of clarity, and feelings of emptiness or despair.

Healing the Crown Chakra

- **Meditation:** Practicing mindfulness or deep meditation can help open and balance the Crown Chakra. Guided meditation focused on higher consciousness or the divine can be especially beneficial.

- **Spiritual Practice:** Engaging in spiritual practices such as prayer, yoga, or connecting with nature can help align and balance this chakra.

- **Aromatherapy:** Essential oils like lavender, frankincense, and sandalwood can promote clarity and spiritual awareness, helping to open the Crown Chakra.

- **Crystals:** Stones such as amethyst, clear quartz, and selenite are commonly used to balance the Crown Chakra. Holding or placing these crystals near the top of the head during meditation can support healing.

Spiritual Significance

In many spiritual traditions, the Crown Chakra is seen as the bridge between the physical and the spiritual and is the gateway to enlightenment or the ultimate state of consciousness. When the Crown Chakra is open, individuals experience a deep connection to the universe and are often guided by a sense of divine purpose.

Chakra System and the Crown

The Crown Chakra is the final point in the sequence of chakras and represents the highest level of spiritual development. It's often considered the "goal" of chakra work because it represents spiritual awakening and ultimate understanding.

When the Crown Chakra is balanced, it integrates the energies of the other chakras, enabling an individual to live in harmony with both their inner self and the universe.

In essence, the Crown Chakra is the center of spiritual wisdom, unity, and divine connection. Healing and balancing this chakra can lead to a profound sense of peace, joy, and spiritual fulfillment.

Crystals

- **Clear Quartz:** Amplifies spiritual connection, clarity, and enlightenment. It's a powerful all-purpose healer.
- **Selenite**: Clears energy blockages, purifies the aura, and enhances spiritual awareness.
- **Amethyst:** Supports meditation, spiritual growth, and connection to higher consciousness.

How to use: Place the crystal at the top of your head or hold it while meditating to enhance your connection with the universe.

How to unblock it:

- **Visualization:** Imagine a violet light radiating from the top of your head, connecting you to the universe.

- **Meditation:** Focus on the stillness within you.

- **Affirmations**: "I am connected to the universe. I am one with all."

- **Nature immersion:** Spend time in nature to feel the unity of all life.

SUGGESTED MEDITATION

- Shift your focus to the top of your head.
- Picture a radiant violet or white light, like a halo of light connecting you to the universe.
- Ask yourself: "Do I feel connected to a higher purpose or spiritual source?"
- If this chakra feels dim, visualize the light expanding upwards, connecting you to the vastness of the universe. Let it fill you with a sense of peace and oneness.
- Affirmation: "I am connected to the divine. I am one with the universe."

The meditations provided in this book are just examples. Feel free to customize them to your personal needs and consciousness expansion. You are growing and changing, so too your meditations will grow as well. You will notice your visualization and guides will help you.

Crown Chakra Foods

The foods that nourish the Crown Chakra are often light, high in energy, and spiritually uplifting. Here are some foods and dietary practices that can help balance and support the Crown Chakra:

1. High-Vibrational Foods - foods that are naturally high in life force energy can support the Crown Chakra. These foods are often light, pure, and spiritually cleansing:

- **Fruits**: Especially those that are fresh, organic, and high in water content. Examples include:
- **Grapes** (especially red or purple varieties, as the color is associated with the Crown Chakra)
- **Berries** (blueberries, blackberries, raspberries)
- **Pomegranates** (symbolizing spiritual rebirth and enlightenment)
- **Apples** (often associated with higher wisdom)
- **Plums and raisins** (for higher consciousness and transformation)
- **Vegetables**: Light, organic, and nutrient-dense vegetables, especially those that promote mental clarity and energy flow. Examples include:
  - **Leafy greens** (spinach, kale, lettuce).
  - **Cauliflower and broccoli** (for their purifying and detoxifying properties).
  - **Sprouts** (high-energy foods that are packed with life force).
  - **Cucumbers and celery** (light, hydrating, and cleansing).

2. **Foods that are White or Violet in Color** - the color associations for the Crown Chakra are white and violet, so incorporating foods that reflect these colors can help energize this chakra:
   - **Garlic and onions** (can purify and detoxify the mind and spirit).
   - **Mushrooms** (especially white varieties like button mushrooms, as they have grounding properties).
   - **Purple foods:** Eggplants, purple cabbage, purple grapes, and purple sweet potatoes (purple helps stimulate spiritual awareness).
   - **Coconut** (the coconut fruit, coconut water, and coconut oil are known for their high vibrational properties).

3. **Herbs and Spices** - Certain herbs and spices can stimulate the Crown Chakra and help you feel more spiritually connected. Examples include:
   - **Saffron**: A sacred and highly spiritual herb that enhances spiritual awareness.
   - **Lavender:** Often used for meditation and relaxation, it can help you feel more centered and peaceful.
   - **Holy Basil** (Tulsi): Known for its uplifting and calming effects, helping to promote clarity of mind and spiritual health.
   - **Frankincense** (in the form of essential oils or as an incense, though not directly a food, it's often used during meals or spiritual practices).

4. **Nuts and Seeds** - Some nuts and seeds are known for their grounding and high-frequency energy, which can help elevate the Crown Chakra:
   - **Almonds:** Known for their connection to the divine and spiritual awakening.
   - **Flaxseeds and chia seeds:** These seeds are packed with omega-3 fatty acids, which support brain function and mental clarity.
   - **Walnuts**: Symbolic of the brain and intelligence, walnuts support mental clarity and focus, which can enhance spiritual practice.
   **One of my personal favorites as it is a natural dewormer as well.

5. Purified Water & Herbal Teas
- **Water:** Pure water is a vital element for cleansing and balancing the Crown Chakra. Hydration supports clarity and mental focus. Drinking water mindfully can be a spiritual practice that helps ground the Crown Chakra.
- **Herbal teas:** Teas such as chamomile, lavender, or green tea can help calm the mind and open the pathways to spiritual awareness.

6. Light, Airy, and Clean Foods
- The Crown Chakra thrives on foods that are light and not overly heavy or greasy. Avoid overly processed foods or foods that are dense and rich in fats or sugars.
- Eating fresh, organic, and minimally processed foods is beneficial for maintaining a high frequency, as they support spiritual clarity and a sense of inner peace.

7. Fermented Foods (In Moderation) - Kimchi, sauerkraut, and miso can help promote gut health, which in turn supports mental clarity and a balanced mind. A balanced mind is essential for connecting to the higher self and divine consciousness.

8. Cleansing Foods - Foods that help detoxify and cleanse the body can also help balance the Crown Chakra, as they promote a sense of purity and spiritual openness.
- Lemon (especially when consumed in water)
- Ginger (helpful for stimulating the digestive system and aiding in purification)
- Cleansing leafy greens, such as parsley or cilantro, can help detoxify both the body and the mind.

9. Fasting or Light Eating Practices - The Crown Chakra thrives when the body is not burdened by excessive, heavy food. Many people who practice spiritual discipline may choose to eat lighter meals, or even fast occasionally, to enhance their connection with higher consciousness. This can create space for spiritual clarity and insight.

By incorporating these foods and practices into your diet, you can support the health and vitality of your Crown Chakra, enhancing your spiritual growth, clarity, and connection to the divine.

Again, take what resonates with you and discard the rest.

If you don't have access to a lavender field, go on a meditation and ask your guides to take you to a beautiful field ... use your senses to start smelling the fragrance and hearing the bees...the magic is within you!

Grounding Healing Powers Revealed

What Is Grounding (Earthing)?
Grounding, also known as earthing, is a practice that involves reconnecting your body to the Earth's natural energy. This can be as simple as walking barefoot on grass, soil, sand, or immersing yourself in natural water sources like oceans or lakes.

The idea is that direct contact with the Earth allows your body to absorb its natural electromagnetic energy, which can have a wide range of health benefits.

The Earth's surface carries a negative electrical charge that can neutralize free radicals in the body, helping reduce inflammation and promote overall well-being.

Scientific Evidence: What Doctors and Research Show
While grounding is not yet mainstream in medical practice, there's a growing body of scientific evidence suggesting that it can have a positive impact on health. Here's a summary of what research has shown:

- **Reduces Inflammation and Pain** - A study published in the journal of Inflammation Research found that grounding can reduce chronic inflammation, which is linked to various diseases like arthritis, heart disease, and diabetes. The theory is that electrons from the Earth's surface can act as antioxidants, neutralizing free radicals that cause inflammation.

- **Improves Sleep and Reduces Stress** - Research published in the Journal of Environmental and Public Health showed that grounding can help regulate cortisol levels (the stress hormone), leading to improved sleep quality. Participants reported feeling less stressed and more relaxed after grounding.

- **Enhances Mood and Reduces Anxiety** - A study by the Journal of Alternative and Complementary Medicine found that grounding can improve mood and reduce symptoms of anxiety and depression. The Earth's energy may help stabilize the body's circadian rhythms, contributing to a calmer state of mind.

- **Lowers Blood Pressure and Supports Heart Health** - Grounding has been linked to improved blood flow and reduced blood viscosity (thickness). A study found that grounding can reduce the risk of cardiovascular disease by helping blood flow more freely, thus lowering blood pressure and reducing the risk of clots.

- **Accelerates Wound Healing** - A clinical study on patients recovering from surgery showed that grounding helped accelerate wound healing, likely due to its effects on reducing inflammation and improving circulation.

- **Boosts Immune Function** - By neutralizing free radicals and reducing inflammation, grounding may support the immune system. Some studies suggest that grounding can enhance the body's ability to fight off infections and illnesses.

How Does Grounding Work?
The Earth has a slightly negative charge due to its abundance of free electrons. The human body, especially in modern environments, can accumulate positive charges due to exposure to electromagnetic fields (EMFs) from electronics, Wi-Fi, and other sources.

Grounding allows free electrons from the Earth to flow into your body, neutralizing positive charges and reducing inflammation.

Orgonites are another substitute to block EMF.

How to Effectively Ground Yourself: Practical Methods
Grounding can be done in a variety of ways, both outdoors and indoors. Here are some of the most effective techniques:

- **Walking Barefoot Outdoors**
    - Why It Works: This allows your body to directly absorb the Earth's electrons. Try doing this for at least 20-30 minutes a day to experience benefits.

- **Grounding in Water [Swimming or immerse your feet]**.
    - Why It Works: Water is a natural conductor of the Earth's energy, making it an excellent way to ground yourself.

- **Using Grounding Mats and Sheets Indoors -** Use specially designed grounding mats, sheets, or bands that connect to a grounded outlet in your home.
    - Why It Works: These products simulate the effects of being directly in contact with the Earth, making grounding accessible indoors.

- **Gardening and Touching Plants -** Simply dig your hands into the soil while gardening or simply spend time touching plants and trees.
    - Why It Works: Direct contact with the Earth while gardening can help you absorb its healing energy, reducing stress and enhancing your mood.

- **Sitting or Lying on the Ground** - Sit or lie down on the ground, preferably on grass, sand, or soil. Ensure as much of your skin as possible is in contact with the Earth.
    - Why It Works: This can be especially effective for calming the mind, reducing stress, and promoting relaxation.

- **Grounding Meditation** - Visualize roots growing from your feet into the Earth while sitting quietly with your feet on the ground. Imagine drawing in the Earth's energy through these roots.
    - This helps you connect mentally and energetically to the Earth's stabilizing energy, promoting a sense of balance.

Tips for Effective Grounding
- **Choose Natural Surfaces**: Grounding works best on natural surfaces like grass, sand, soil, or unsealed concrete. Asphalt, wood, or synthetic surfaces do not conduct the Earth's energy effectively.

- **Be Consistent**: For the best results, practice grounding regularly. Even just a few minutes a day can have cumulative benefits.

- **Pay Attention to Your Body**: Notice how you feel before and after grounding sessions. You may experience increased calm, better focus, or relief from pain.

- **Practice Mindfulness**: Combine grounding with deep breathing, meditation, or mindful walking to enhance the effects.

- **Hydrate**: Staying hydrated can improve your body's ability to conduct energy, making grounding more effective.

The Benefits of Grounding - Grounding is a simple yet powerful practice that can benefit both your physical and mental health. By taking time each day to connect with the Earth's natural energy, you can reduce stress, improve your sleep, and support overall well-being and enhance your health.

Ever wonder why your cat or dogs love laying in the grass?

Animals' Healing Powers & Grounding

Grounding for Animals: Benefits and Techniques

Grounding, also known as earthing, is not just beneficial for humans—our animal companions can also benefit greatly from connecting to the Earth's natural energy.

Just like us, animals are sensitive to the electromagnetic fields (EMFs) in their environment, and grounding can help restore balance to their bodies, reduce stress, and improve overall health.

Whether it's your pet dog, cat, horse, or even smaller animals like rabbits, grounding can have a calming and healing effect. Here's a deeper look into how grounding benefits animals and how you can practice grounding with them.

Benefits of Grounding for Animals

- **Reduces Stress and Anxiety -** Just like humans, animals can experience stress and anxiety from their environment, especially when exposed to EMFs from household electronics, Wi-Fi, and other modern devices. Grounding can help calm their nervous system, promoting a sense of peace and relaxation. This is particularly helpful for pets with anxiety issues, especially during stressful events like thunderstorms, fireworks, or travel.

- **Relieves Pain and Inflammation -** Grounding can help reduce inflammation in animals, which is particularly beneficial for pets with arthritis, joint pain, or injuries. By absorbing the Earth's free electrons, animals can experience relief from chronic pain and faster recovery from injuries.

- **Improves Sleep and Restfulness** - Grounding can help regulate your pet's circadian rhythm, leading to better sleep. This is especially useful for pets who are restless or have trouble sleeping through the night.

- **Boosts Immunity and Overall Health** - Connecting with the Earth's energy may enhance your pet's immune function, making them less prone to illness. Regular grounding can support better digestion, healthier skin, and improved vitality, contributing to a longer, healthier life.
- **Promotes Emotional Balance** - Animals are highly sensitive to their surroundings and can pick up on the emotions of their owners. Grounding can help them release emotional stress and restore emotional balance.
    - This is especially helpful for rescue animals or pets who have experienced trauma or abuse.

Effective Grounding Techniques for Animals

Here are some simple and effective ways to ground your pets:

- **Walk Barefoot with Your Pets on Natural Surfaces** - Simply take your dog for a walk on grass, dirt, or sand. Allow them to walk barefoot (paw pads directly touching the ground) to naturally connect with the Earth.
    - **Benefits:** Walking on natural surfaces not only grounds your pet but also provides them with exercise and mental stimulation.
- **Let Your Pets Lie on the Ground** - Let your pets spend time lying directly on grass, soil, or sand. Encourage them to rest outdoors where they can fully connect to the Earth's energy.
    - **Benefits**: This is especially good for older pets who may suffer from arthritis or joint pain. The Earth's energy can help reduce inflammation and provide comfort.
- **Use Grounding Mats or Pads Indoors** - Place a grounding mat where your pet likes to sleep or relax indoors. These mats are designed to mimic the grounding effect of natural surfaces by connecting to a grounded outlet.
    - **Benefits**: This is ideal for pets who spend most of their time indoors or live in urban environments where natural grounding surfaces are limited.

- **Pet Massage While Grounded** - Sit with your pet outdoors on the grass. Use gentle massage techniques, focusing on areas where your pet may hold tension, like the shoulders or hips.
    - **Benefits:** This not only helps with bonding but also allows both you and your pet to ground together, enhancing the calming effect.

- **Let Them Dig or Roll in the Dirt -** Encourage your dog to dig or allow your cat to roll in the dirt in a safe outdoor space. Letting animals connect with the Earth through their natural instincts can be very grounding.
    - **Benefits:** Animals instinctively know that being close to the Earth helps them release stress and recharge.

It is my observation that animals are lightholders that, in their natural state, animals embody spiritual light, wisdom, and healing energy. Whether through their role as spiritual guides, their healing presence, or their connection to the natural and divine worlds, animals serve as vessels of higher consciousness, helping us reconnect with our own innate light.

By simply being themselves, animals teach us profound lessons on living in harmony with nature, experiencing unconditional love, and embracing universal wisdom.

Their ability to love without judgment, expectation, or condition is, in my view, their greatest gift — showing us the purest form of love and reminding us of the deep spiritual bond we share with all living beings.

In my experience, every new horse we've rescued over the years has done the same thing. As soon as they are released into their new grass pasture, they run to the middle of the field, flop onto their backs, and roll with all four legs in the air. It's magical to watch these 2,000-pound horses roll in the grass, bathed in the light of day.

Grounding as a Natural Healing Practice for Animals

Just like humans, animals can greatly benefit from reconnecting with the Earth's natural energy.

Grounding is a simple, cost-effective, and natural way to support your pet's physical and emotional well-being. Whether it's allowing your pet to walk barefoot, lie on the grass, or use a grounding mat indoors, these practices can improve their health, reduce anxiety, and enhance their quality of life.

So, the next time you take your dog for a walk or let your cat explore the backyard, remember that you're not just giving them exercise—you're helping them ground and heal in a way that's natural and beneficial.

- I love taking my dog for walks around the farm. I'll pick fresh, wild chives and absorb their fragrance. I find they alert my senses, focus and makes me happy.

- You too can discover and explore mindful techniques help you rebalance and grow. Remember to write them in your journal when you discover them.

Have you ever noticed how much our pets love to sunbathe? Even indoors, they seek out a sunny spot by a window, stretching out to soak up the rays.

Cats and dogs are sentient beings, capable of experiencing emotions, forming connections, and responding to their environment in meaningful ways. They have unique personalities and awareness, making them much more than just pets—they are conscious, feeling creatures.

Trees' Magical Healing Benefits

Benefits of Trees and Grounding

Connecting with Nature's Energy - Trees are powerful, natural healers that play a significant role in grounding. By connecting with trees, we can harness their stable, grounding energy to balance our bodies, minds, and spirits. Trees are deeply rooted in the Earth, allowing them to draw up and store the Earth's natural energy, which they can share with us through touch and proximity.

Grounding with trees involves connecting with their energy to release stress, improve physical health, and cultivate inner peace. Let's explore the benefits of tree-grounding, along with techniques to practice it effectively.

Benefits of Grounding with Trees

- **Reduces Stress and Anxiety:**
    - Spending time near trees has been shown to lower cortisol levels (the stress hormone) and promote relaxation.
    - Tree grounding can provide a calming effect on the nervous system, helping to reduce anxiety and promote emotional well-being.

- **Improves Mental Clarity and Focus:**
    - The presence of trees and nature improves concentration and mental clarity. Studies show that spending time in nature can boost cognitive function and creativity.
    - Grounding with trees helps quiet the mind, making it easier to focus on the present moment.

- **Balances Energy and Emotions:**
    - Trees are natural conductors of the Earth's energy. Connecting with them can help balance your energy field, reduce negative emotions, and promote a sense of inner peace.
    - Tree grounding can help release pent-up emotions, leaving you feeling lighter and more centered.

Strengthens the Immune System

- Trees release phytoncides, natural compounds that can boost the immune system. Spending time in forests or near trees can enhance immunity and overall health.

- Grounding with trees helps align your body's energy, promoting healing and rejuvenation.

- Enhances Grounding and Connection to the Earth

Trees are deeply rooted, symbolizing stability, strength, and resilience. Grounding with trees can help you feel more anchored, balanced, and connected to the Earth.
By touching or sitting near trees, you can absorb their stabilizing energy, which can help you feel more grounded in your daily life.

Techniques for Grounding with Trees
1. Tree Hugging - Approach a tree that resonates with you. Stand close to it, take a few deep breaths, and gently place your arms around its trunk. Rest your forehead or cheek against the bark if you feel comfortable.

- **Benefits:** As you hug the tree, imagine it absorbing any stress or negative energy from your body and replacing it with a sense of calm and stability. *Tip*: Focus on feeling the tree's energy flowing into your body.

2. Standing or sitting with Your Back Against a Tree - Stand with your back pressed against the trunk of a tree. Close your eyes, take deep breaths, and focus on the sensation of the tree supporting you.

- **Benefits**: This position allows you to align your spine with the tree, helping to balance your energy and calm your mind.
- **Visualization**: Imagine the tree's roots extending deep into the Earth and drawing up energy. Visualize this energy traveling up through the tree into your body.

3. Sitting at the Base of a Tree for Meditation - Find a comfortable spot at the base of a tree. Sit with your spine straight, your back gently touching the trunk, and your feet resting on the ground.

- **Benefits:** This technique is excellent for grounding during meditation. The tree acts as an anchor, helping to calm your mind and connect you to the Earth's energy.
- **Guided Visualization:** As you meditate, visualize the tree's energy flowing through your spine, grounding you and clearing your energy field.

4. Touching the Bark with Your Hands - Stand or sit near a tree and place both hands on the trunk. Focus on the texture of the bark, the temperature, and the feeling of connection.

- **Benefits:** Touching the bark helps you tune into the tree's energy. It can be a quick way to ground yourself if you're feeling anxious or disconnected.
- **Breathwork:** As you breathe deeply, imagine any stress leaving your body through your hands and being absorbed by the tree.

5. Walking Barefoot Among Trees
Find a park, forest, or garden where you can walk barefoot on natural ground among trees. Focus on feeling the Earth beneath your feet and the energy of the trees around you.

Mindfulness Practice: Pay attention to the sounds, scents, and sights around you. Let your mind relax as you connect with nature.

Tree-Grounding Visualization Technique - Here's a simple visualization you can practice enhancing your grounding experience with trees:

- **Find a Quiet Spot Near a Tree**: Sit or stand near a tree, close your eyes, and take a few deep breaths to relax.
- **Visualize Roots Growing from Your Feet:** Imagine roots extending from the soles of your feet deep into the Earth, connecting you to the tree's roots.
- **Feel the Energy Flow:** Picture energy from the Earth flowing up through the tree's roots, into the trunk, and then into your body through your feet or hands.
- **Release Tension**: As you breathe out, imagine releasing any tension, stress, or negative emotions into the tree. The tree will transform this energy into positive, healing energy.
- **Fill with Light:** On your inhale, imagine drawing in pure, golden light from the Earth, filling your entire body with healing energy.
- **Express Gratitude:** Before ending, thank the tree for sharing its grounding energy with you.

Tips for Effective Tree Grounding
- **Choose the Right Tree:** Spend some time intuitively selecting a tree that you feel drawn to. Different trees have different energies—some are grounding, while others are more uplifting.
- **Be Consistent**: For the best results, practice grounding with trees regularly, even if it's just a few minutes each day.
- **Respect Nature:** Always treat trees and nature with respect. Ask for permission (silently or aloud) before engaging with a tree, and express gratitude afterward.

Solar Flares & Healing

The Connection Between Solar Flares and Healing the Human Body

Currently, the sun is consistently firing off the strongest solar flares we have experienced in which science measures as an X class flare, falling into the category of the most intense levels of solar explosions.

Coronal Mass Ejections (CMEs) are bursts of charged particles and magnetic energy released from the Sun, similar to a volcanic eruption. When these bursts reach Earth, they interact with our planet's ionosphere, causing changes in the magnetic field and triggering geomagnetic storms, auroras, and an increase in the Earth's plasma fountain.

This phenomenon is clear evidence that we are experiencing a powerful Solar Initiation, with radiating plasmic light that is rapidly influencing humanity's evolution — or digression — on our spiritual journey here on Earth.

We are moving into the next stage of planetary consciousness because of a shift in the timelines or "time fields." This shift is creating a new phase of evolution for the planet and its collective energy.

This is a magnetic shift happening between different timelines that guide humanity's evolution and future direction on Earth.

Think of it like a galactic "superhighway" that connects to the planet's energy system, functioning like an interdimensional routing network. Humanity is now at a crucial turning point, where we must choose the vibration of our spiritual path. This choice will determine the overall energy of our future. We're at a crossroads: we can either move toward our highest potential and a positive future or fall into a negative one.

How Solar Flares May Affect the Human Body

Though the scientific community is still researching the full effects of solar flares on human health, if you're reading this book, you know that these solar events can influence our physical, emotional, and energetic systems in various ways:

Electromagnetic Sensitivity

The human body is an electromagnetic system; our cells, nervous system, and even our heart emit electromagnetic fields.

Solar flares can disrupt Earth's magnetic field, which in turn may affect our own bioelectric fields. Some people report experiencing symptoms such as headaches, fatigue, anxiety, or even palpitations during times of heightened solar activity.

Impact on the Pineal Gland

The pineal gland, sometimes called the "third eye," is sensitive to electromagnetic energy. It is responsible for regulating sleep-wake cycles, melatonin production, and even spiritual experiences.

Solar flares are believed to stimulate the pineal gland, potentially enhancing intuition, clarity, and spiritual insight. This is why some people feel more awake, alert, or spiritually tuned in during solar flares.

DNA Activation and Cellular Healing

Some holistic health practitioners believe that the energy from solar flares can "activate" dormant parts of our DNA, promoting healing and cellular regeneration.

The theory suggests that the high-frequency energy from solar flares can trigger a kind of energetic reset in the body, helping cells to repair and heal.

Emotional and Mental Effects

Increased solar activity can heighten emotions, leading to mood swings, anxiety, or feelings of overwhelm. However, it can also promote heightened awareness, creativity, and inspiration.

Some people report feeling a surge of energy, increased motivation, or an urge to make positive changes in their lives during solar flare events.

Solar Flares and Spiritual Awakening

Many spiritual communities believe that solar flares play a role in spiritual awakening and consciousness expansion. Here's how:

- **Energetic Upgrades:** Solar flares are believed to trigger energy shifts that can help cleanse and align the body's chakras, promote emotional release, and facilitate spiritual growth.

- **Increased Intuition:** The energetic influx can enhance psychic abilities, such as intuition, telepathy, or even lucid dreaming. This can open up new levels of consciousness.

- **Emotional Release:** Solar flares may help release deeply buried emotions, allowing you to heal old wounds and move forward with greater clarity and purpose.

1. How to Harness Solar Flares for Healing - If you are interested in using solar flares for healing and spiritual growth, here are some techniques you can try:

- **Refer back the Grounding and Earthing Section -** This helps ground your energy and balance the effects of heightened electromagnetic activity.
    - **Benefits**: Grounding can help reduce feelings of anxiety, restlessness, and fatigue that may arise during solar flares.

2. Meditate and Tune Into the Energy - Find a quiet place to meditate during solar flares. Focus on your breath and visualize absorbing the sun's energy to cleanse and heal your body.

- **Benefits**: Meditation can help you integrate the energy from solar flares, leading to enhanced clarity, spiritual insights, and a sense of inner peace.

3. Use Crystals for Protection and Healing - Suggested Crystals: Carry these crystals with you or place them in your home during times of heightened solar activity to protect your energy field.

- **Black Tourmaline**: For grounding and protection against electromagnetic fields.
- **Selenite**: For clearing energy blockages and enhancing spiritual connection.
- **Amethyst**: For calming the mind, enhancing intuition, and connecting with higher consciousness.

4. Drink Plenty of Water - Solar flares can increase the body's need for hydration. Drinking plenty of water helps flush out toxins and supports your body's ability to adjust to the new energies.

- Avoid city water - fluoride calcifies your pineal gland and impedes your ascension.
- Fresh fruits are a great source of water and contain antioxidants.
- **Tip**: Add a pinch of CELTIC salt or lemon juice to your water to enhance its conductivity and improve cellular hydration.

5. Practice Deep Breathing and Energy Cleansing - Practice slow, deep breathing exercises to help regulate your nervous system. Imagine each inhale filling you with healing energy from the sun, and each exhale releasing any negative energy.

- **Benefits**: This can help calm your mind, reduce stress, and improve your body's ability to integrate solar energies.

Embracing the Energy of Solar Flares for Healing

While the effects of solar flares on the human body are still being studied, many people report feeling significant shifts during periods of increased solar activity. By using grounding techniques, meditation, and holistic practices, you can harness the power of solar flares to support your physical, emotional, and spiritual well-being.

If our personal DNA is not in alignment with the Earth's natural energy, it can prevent us from accessing important species memories or "ascension codes" stored in the Earth's energy.

As we commit to living in alignment with our highest spiritual expression, we are constantly exposed to higher energy frequencies and light symbols. These light symbols activate the Crystal Body, helping us channel energy, light, and sound into new patterns that influence our DNA. Light symbols may appear as shapes like Platonic solids or as light language, forming complex patterns that carry instructions. These codes guide the energy within the grids of light and sound that shape our reality.

These new DNA patterns, often described as "musical tones," help unlock higher potentials within our DNA, prompting changes in our physical body. These "musical tones" are signals that organize the components of DNA, such as nucleotides and protein chains, and repair our damaged DNA.

Remember that the energy from solar flares is a natural part of the universe's rhythm. Learning to flow with this energy can help you embrace change, enhance your intuition, and even accelerate your personal healing and spiritual journey.

Tip: Sunscreen is dangerous, avoid it at all costs. Always review the labels and research what you are lathering on your body. Your skin is your largest organ.

This process involves re-organizing the crystalline matrix in our body, where solar energy activates plasma crystals in the web of our nervous system. This helps upgrade the cells in our bones, blood, skin, and tissues to receive new liquid plasma energy codes.

This is an integral part of activating your light body.

This is what it means to INTEGRATE your higher self.

It doesn't matter how others see you - it only matters HOW YOU SEE YOURSELF!

Bioplasma Cell Salts
STARSEEDS' SUPPLEMENT

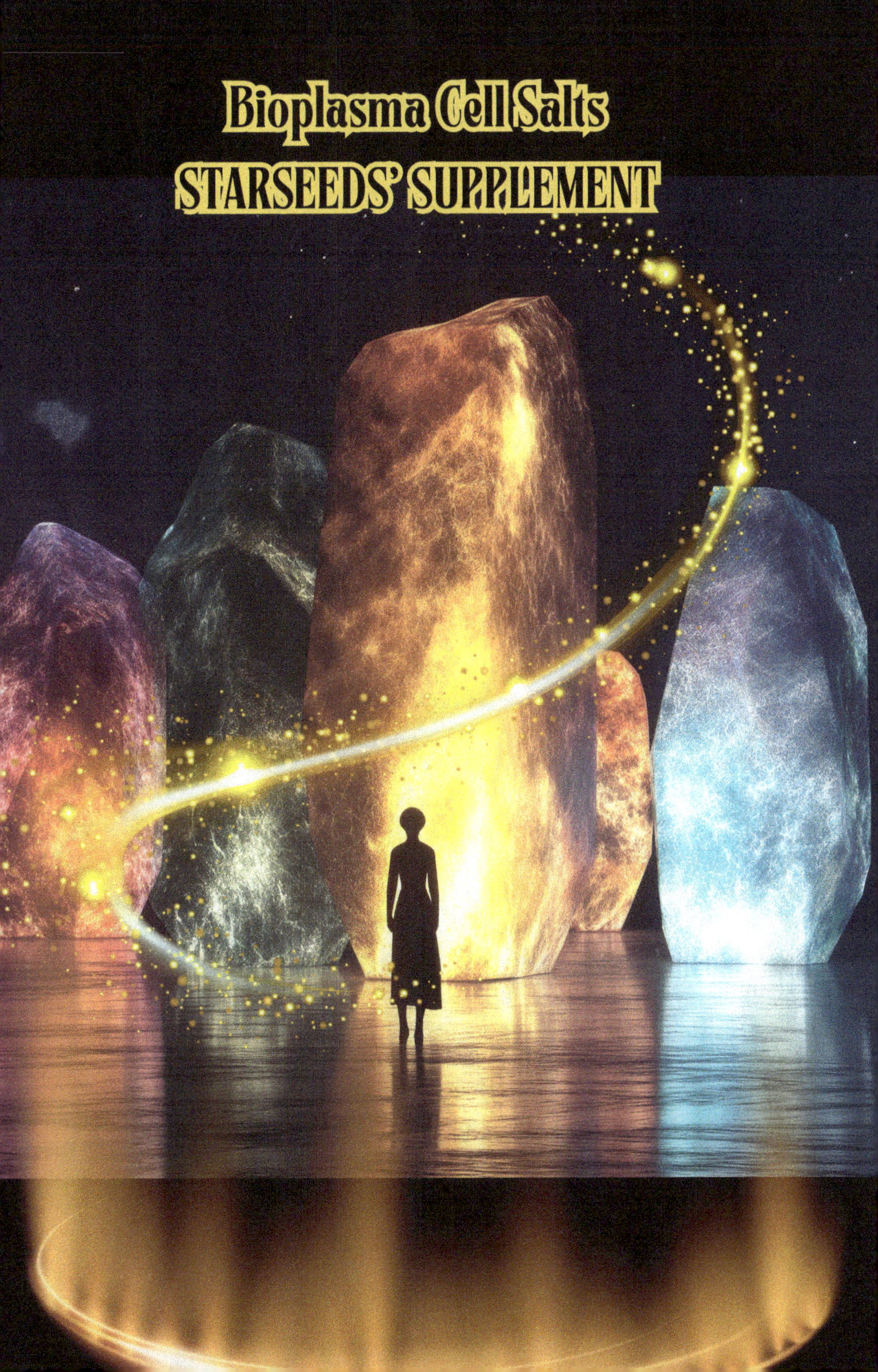

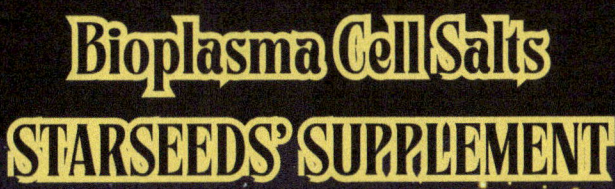

The 12 Biochemic Salts

Ancient Mystery Schools, like those in Alexandria, Egypt, and Greece, understood the importance of mineral cell salts in spiritual initiation, particularly in the process of Hieros Gamos (sacred union). This process allows higher frequencies to be embodied by nourishing the cells with the mineral energy needed for transformation.

Tissue salts are made up of natural elements already present in the body. They are the building blocks of our cells, tissues, and organs, and the body uses their energy for essential metabolic functions.

Dr. W.H. Scheussler's Biochemic Theory is the foundation of the Hyland's Cell Salts of Life

Dr. Schuessler identified 12 different Cell Salts that are present in every cell of the human body. He discovered that when cells become deficient in one or more of these salts, specific symptoms appear. By replacing the missing Bio Salt(s), the symptoms can be relieved quickly.

Dr. Schuessler's biochemical system has proven effective over time because it works. You don't need professional training to use cell salts — anyone can benefit from this pioneering research. Simply pay attention to the symptoms in your body, mind, and emotions to guide you in choosing the right salt.

This is a safe and effective step toward self-healing. There is no toxicity, and if you take the wrong Bio Cell Salt, it simply won't have any effect.

BioChemical Cell Salts can safely help you find the right salts for your specific symptoms. Keep track of the treatments that work for you.

Each salt addresses specific deficiencies and promotes overall health by ensuring cells receive the necessary nutrients to repair and maintain themselves. They are believed to treat a wide range of conditions, from minor ailments to chronic diseases, by addressing the root cause rather than just masking symptoms

- **Note: BioChemical Cell Salts are not homeopathically made but are naturally found in the body.**
    - They should not be confused with homeopathic remedies, which are made from substances not typically found in the body and may cause symptoms when taken in higher doses.
    - Unlike BioChemical Cell Salts, homeopathic remedies work similarly to pharmaceuticals, but in a diluted, natural form.

Between 1872 and 1898, Dr. Schuessler discovered that 12 mineral tissue salts were essential for health: Calc Fluor, Calc Phos, Calc Sulph, Ferr Phos, Kali Mur, Kali Phos, Kali Sulph, Mag Phos, Nat Mur, Nat Phos, Nat Sulph, and Silica.

A deficiency in any of these salts weakens cell structure and causes illness. When the deficiency is corrected, the cells return to normal function and health is restored. Biochemic tissue salts, also known as cell salts, are minerals in an energy form.

Dr. Schuessler's therapy finds confirmation through the statement of Noble Prize winner Dr. Linus Pauling:

"You can trace every sickness, every disease and every ailment to a mineral deficiency."

Dr. Wilhelm Schuessler, the German physician who pioneered the concept of cell salts, developed his system in the 19th century (around 1872).

For a time, tissue salts were widely used in natural and homeopathic healing practices, but as the pharmaceutical industry grew and more conventional drugs were developed, there was a shift toward more synthetic, chemical-based treatments.

Cell salts can be taken in tablet form and are often used in combination to address specific health concerns. They work by supporting cellular function and helping to restore balance in the body.

By the early 1900s, with the rise of Big Pharma and the increasing dominance of allopathic (conventional) medicine, more natural remedies like cell salts were overshadowed.

Cell salts, also known as tissue salts or Biochemic salts, were not exactly "removed" by Big Pharma, but they became less prominent in mainstream medical practices as pharmaceuticals and more modern forms of medicine gained popularity in the late 19th and early 20th centuries.

Big Pharm - the financial performance of big pharmaceuticals revealed:

- $1.55 TRILLION USD in total revenue in 2023.
- $1.6 TRILLION USD are total revenue projections in 2024.

Do you see based on facts why the natural remedies were suppressed from the public?

The 12 Biochemic Salts and how to use them today:

Cell salts deficiencies tend to show up first in the face because the skin there is thinner, more sensitive, and has a rich blood supply, making it more responsive to internal imbalances.

- The face also has a higher rate of cellular turnover, so when mineral deficiencies occur, they manifest more quickly. Additionally, the facial muscles are highly active, and mineral imbalances can lead to issues like sagging, wrinkles, or dull skin.

- The skin is often seen as a mirror of internal health, and when the body is deficient in essential minerals, it prioritizes other bodily functions over skin health, leading to visible signs like dryness, acne, or discoloration, especially in the face.

- The face is also connected to reflex zones that correspond to various organs, so deficiencies in minerals affecting these organs often result in localized skin changes. Certain cell salts, like Silicea (for collagen production) and Calcium Fluoride (for skin elasticity), play key roles in skin health.

- When these salts are deficient, symptoms like dryness, wrinkles, or puffiness are common. The face's direct exposure to environmental factors, combined with its sensitivity to hydration and electrolyte balance, makes it the first place to show the effects of mineral imbalances, highlighting the body's need for cell salts to restore balance.

Biochemical cell salts are made like this:
Mineral Selection: Choose essential minerals like calcium, magnesium, potassium, and iron needed for cellular health.
Trituration: Grind the selected minerals with lactose powder in a specific ratio (usually 1 part mineral to 9 parts lactose).
Serial Dilution and Succussion & Tableting
This method helps ensure the minerals are in a form that can be easily absorbed by the body's cells, supporting overall health and healing.

What Are Bioplasma Cell Salts?

- Bioplasma cell salts, also known as tissue salts or Schüssler salts, are a set of mineral compounds that were developed in the 19th century by Dr. Wilhelm Heinrich Schüssler, a German physician.

- They are based on the idea that disease is caused by imbalances or deficiencies in the body's mineral levels. These salts are believed to support cellular function and promote overall health by restoring these mineral balances.

- Bioplasma, specifically, is a combination of all 12 cell salts formulated to work synergistically to maintain and improve cellular health. It is often used as a general tonic to boost vitality, improve resilience, and support the body's natural healing processes.

Together all 12 of these mineral cell salts combined are called Bioplasma.

- In our spiritual community the necessity of soothing the brain and nervous system from exhaustion during many Ascension Symptoms have given Bioplasma the nickname of the "Starseed Supplement".

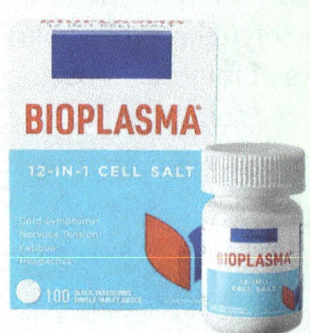

This brand is most known and available on Amazon.com. The pills just melt in your mouth with no side effects because they are ALL NATURAL.

Choose a brand that resonates with you.

The 12 Cell Salts Included in Bioplasma

- **Calcarea Fluorica (Calcium Fluoride)** - Supports elasticity in tissues, bones, and teeth.
- **Calcarea Phosphorica (Calcium Phosphate)** - Aids bone growth and repair, especially in children.
- **Calcarea Sulphurica (Calcium Sulphate)** - Helps with skin health and healing of wounds.
- **Ferrum Phosphoricum (Iron Phosphate)** - Boosts oxygen transport, reduces inflammation, and improves immunity.
- **Kali Muriaticum (Potassium Chloride)** - Useful for respiratory issues and mucus congestion.
- **Kali Phosphoricum (Potassium Phosphate)** - Supports nerve health, mood, and mental clarity.
- **Kali Sulphuricum (Potassium Sulphate)** - Assists in detoxification and skin health.
- **Magnesia Phosphorica (Magnesium Phosphate)** - Relieves muscle cramps, spasms, and headaches.
- **Natrum Muriaticum (Sodium Chloride)** - Balances fluid levels and helps with emotional health.
- **Natrum Phosphoricum (Sodium Phosphate)** - Alkalizes the body and reduces acidity.
- **Natrum Sulphuricum (Sodium Sulphate)** - Supports liver function and detoxification.
- **Silicea (Silica)** - Strengthens connective tissues, hair, and nails.

Always refer to the specific instructions on the product label or consult a healthcare professional if you're unsure about the dosage or have any concerns.

Tips for Taking Bioplasma Cell Salts:
- Dissolve tablets under the tongue for optimal absorption. This allows the salts to enter the bloodstream more effectively.
- Take on an empty stomach, ideally 30 minutes before or after eating, drinking, or brushing your teeth to ensure better absorption.
- Avoid strong flavors (like coffee, mint, or spicy foods) close to the time of taking cell salts, as these may interfere with their effectiveness.

Precautions:
- While bioplasma cell salts are generally safe, they should be used with caution in pregnant or nursing women, and it's best to consult a healthcare provider.
- People with severe health conditions or those taking prescription medications should also consult a doctor before starting any new supplement, including bioplasma cell salts.

Benefits of Using Cell Salts for Animals

Cell salts can be beneficial for addressing a wide range of issues in animals, such as:

- **Joint and Bone Health:**
  - Calcarea Phosphorica: Supports bone growth and healing, especially in growing puppies or elderly pets with arthritis.
  - Calcarea Fluorica: Helps with joint flexibility and can be beneficial for pets with ligament injuries or arthritis.

- **Digestive Health:**
  - Natrum Phosphoricum: Balances acidity, which can help with digestive issues like acid reflux or diarrhea.
  - Silicea: Supports detoxification and can assist with abscesses or digestive upsets.

- **Skin, Coat, and Wound Healing:**
  - Calcarea Sulphurica: Assists in healing skin conditions like hot spots, wounds, and infections.
  - Kali Sulphuricum: Useful for skin rashes, eczema, and promoting healthy fur growth.
  - Silicea: Helps with skin infections, abscesses, and strengthening nails and hooves.

- **Nervous System and Anxiety:**
  - Kali Phosphoricum: Supports the nervous system, useful for pets with anxiety, stress, or nervousness.
  - Magnesia Phosphorica: Helps relieve muscle spasms and cramps and can calm pets during stressful situations like thunderstorms or fireworks.

- **Respiratory Issues:**
  - Ferrum Phosphoricum: Supports oxygenation and reduces inflammation in the respiratory system, helpful for pets with asthma or respiratory infections.
  - Kali Muriaticum: Assists with mucus buildup, helpful for pets with congestion or sinus issues.

Unlike prescriptions: These remedies are highly diluted and safe for all ages, with no risk of toxicity. They are made without animal testing or animal-derived ingredients, making them a humane and ethical option for those seeking natural remedies.

Dosage Guidelines for Animals 6X potency - The dosage of cell salts for animals is generally based on their size and weight. Here are some general guidelines:

- **Small Animals** (Cats, Small Dogs, Rabbits, etc.)
  - Dosage: 1-2 tablets, 1-3 times a day.
  - Method: Dissolve the tablets in a small amount of water and mix into their food or water bowl. Alternatively, you can place dissolved cell salts into a dropper and give it directly into their mouth.

- **Medium to Large Dogs**
  - Dosage: 2-4 tablets, 1-3 times a day.
  - Method: Dissolve in water or administer directly into their mouth. Tablets can also be crushed and mixed into their food.

- **Horses and Livestock**
  - Dosage: 6-8 tablets, 1-3 times a day.
  - Method: Dissolve in water and mix into feed or administer directly into the mouth using a syringe.

- **Special Considerations**
  - Safety: Cell salts are generally safe and have no known side effects, as they are highly diluted. They can be used alongside conventional veterinary treatments.
  - Natural Mineral Source: Cell salts are derived from naturally occurring minerals essential for cellular health and function.

Consultation: Always consult with a veterinarian, especially if your pet has a serious health condition or is on other medications.

Practical Tips for Administering Cell Salts to Animals
- **Mixing with Food:** If your pet is picky, dissolve the cell salts in a small amount of water and mix it into a treat or wet food.
- **Direct Administration:** For animals that don't mind oral administration, you can dissolve the salts in water and use a dropper to place the liquid directly in their mouth.
- **Avoid Strong Flavors:** Keep the administration away from strong flavors (like mint) that might interfere with the salts' effectiveness.
- Cell salts offer a gentle, holistic approach to support your pet's health, and many animal lovers find them to be an effective complementary treatment.

I rescued a horse from St. Alberta Canada years ago, He was a grey Shire and his hind legs were covered in proud flesh. While granulation tissue is normally part of healing, in cases of proud flesh, it grows excessively, forming a raised, fleshy mass that extends beyond the wound edges.

When he arrived at my farm, the smell of infection was beyond comprehension. His legs were stocked - means so swollen that he had to swing his legs to walk. Moses was the worst case of proud flesh on a horse I'd ever seen. His gut was destroyed from traditional antibiotics. His condition was so severe it required thinking outside the box.

With the help of a homeopathic vet, I was instructed by how to administer cell salts to Moses. I simply diluted the cell salts in water and used a dropper to put in his food. Within a year, the cell salts with the daily cleaning removed much of the proud flesh and he was able to walk without being stiff legged.

Moses retired here on my farm and touched more lives than I can count. Foster kids would finger-paint him, and he loved all the beauty makeovers. His days were filled with meadows, green grass, and the joyful company of foster kids. He never worked another day and peacefully passed away in his sleep in his pasture about five years later, simply due to old age.

I personally witnessed how cell salts healed a horse that escaped slaughter not once, but three times, before finally finding his forever home here on my farm.

Before that experience, I was skeptical about cell salts and unaware of their healing power.

While I'm not a vet, I have a deep love for animals and run a large rescue farm. I always go above and beyond to love, care for, and heal these animals. In return, they give back far more than we could ever offer them.

Publication: "The Draft Horse Journal" Autumn, 2008, "God's Gentle Giants" by Karen L. Kirsch

CRYSTALS REVEALED

This is the starting point to begin making a change and shifting direction. As we transform to a higher level, we are moving into a new time and space.

General Tips for Using Crystals to Unblock Chakras

- **Meditation:** Hold the crystal in your hand or place it on the corresponding chakra during meditation. Focus on your breath and visualize the color of the chakra becoming brighter and more vibrant.
- **Crystal Elixirs:** Place a crystal in a glass of purified water (ensure it is safe for use in water) and leave it in the sunlight for a few hours. Drink the water to absorb the crystal's energy.
- **Wearing Crystals**: Wear crystals as jewelry (bracelets, necklaces, or rings) to keep their energy close to your chakras throughout the day.
- **Sleeping with Crystals:** Place crystals under your pillow or next to your bed to work on balancing your chakras while you sleep.
- **Crystal Grids:** Create a grid using different crystals to balance all your chakras at once. Arrange the crystals in a circle or pattern and sit in the center to soak in their energy.

By integrating these crystals into your daily life, you can gently unblock your chakras and restore balance, allowing your energy to flow freely once again.

Selecting a crystal should be an intuitive experience. Whether you're choosing a crystal for healing, spiritual growth, or simply because you're drawn to it, there are several ways to find one that resonates with you.

Don't overthink it—*often, the crystal that catches your eye or that you feel an inexplicable pull towards is the one meant for you.*

Find an authentic crystal dealer - unfortunately there are many imitations now. Use your intuition to find real ones.

Pay Attention to Color and Appearance - Different crystals are associated with different colors that correspond to the chakras and different types of healing:

1. **Red/Black** (e.g., garnet, obsidian): Grounding, protection, and stability.
2. **Orange/Yellow** (e.g., carnelian, citrine): Confidence, creativity, and motivation.
3. **Green/Pink** (e.g., jade, rose quartz): Emotional healing and love.
4. **Blue/Purple** (e.g., lapis lazuli, amethyst): Communication, intuition, and spiritual growth.

You may feel drawn to certain colors, which can indicate what kind of support you need energetically.

Research the Properties - If you have a specific purpose in mind, research the metaphysical properties of crystals to find one that aligns with your needs. For instance:

1. For stress relief and relaxation, consider amethyst or lepidolite.
2. For manifestation and abundance, citrine or pyrite may be ideal.
3. For protection, look for black tourmaline or smoky quartz.

I started with just a few crystals, but now I have many. In fact, I might need an intervention because my collection has grown so large. Honestly, though, I don't think it's possible to have too many crystals!

If I have sick animal or a new rescue, I always provide them with a rose quartz for healing. It is common for me to place rose quartz in chicken & peacock nests, newly hatchlings and my gardens. My plants love being accessorized!

I turned my greenhouse into a lighthouse for crystals during the off-season months so they can recharge.

How to Clean and Recharge Your Crystals

ALWAYS - Cleanse the Crystal Before Use: Once you've selected a crystal, it's important to cleanse it to clear any energy it may have absorbed before reaching you.

Caring for your crystals is important to keep them energetically clear and effective. Over time, they can absorb energies from their surroundings or from the people who handle them, which can make them less effective. Here are some of the best methods to cleanse and recharge your crystals:

- **Running Water –** Best For: Hard, non-porous crystals like Quartz, Amethyst, and Citrine
    - Hold the crystal under cool, running water (like a stream or tap).
    - As the water flows over the stone, visualize negative energy washing away.
    - Pat dry with a soft cloth or let it air dry.

    Note: *Avoid using this method on soft, porous, or delicate crystals like Selenite, Malachite, or Lapis Lazuli, as water can damage them.*

- **Sea Salt or Saltwater**
    - Fill a bowl with water and dissolve a tablespoon of sea salt and place your crystal in the water for a few hours or overnight, rinse the crystal under clean water afterward and dry it.
    - **Note:** *This method is not recommended for soft or brittle stones*

My go to cleaning is soapy well water, air dry and place in the sun.

- **Sunlight** - Best For: Sun-loving stones like Citrine, Clear Quartz, and Carnelian
    - Place your crystal in direct sunlight for a few hours (morning is best to avoid intense midday heat).
    - The sunlight will recharge your stone with positive energy.
    - **Note:** *Be cautious, as some crystals (e.g., Amethyst, Rose Quartz) can fade in color if left in direct sunlight for too long.*
    - *You can charge in the moonlight, dirt or smudge with sage, but my personal favorite is sunlight.*

NOT COMMONLY KNOWN ABOUT CRYSTALS

Crystals hold the energetic records of Earth's evolutionary history and beyond, storing the experiences and consciousness of all life through complex patterns of frequencies and mathematical codes.

They can amplify and accelerate light frequencies, working like an energy-based software program. Crystals are used for various purposes, such as communication, energy production, teleportation, weather control, and storing vast amounts of frequency-coded information.

Many of us may still carry cellular memories from ancient civilizations like Lemuria, Atlantis, or even earlier root races, such as Tara. We once knew that crystals generated energy fields that formed grid networks, which controlled the holographic field of creation.

After the fall of Atlantis, the knowledge of these crystalline fields and interdimensional gateways was passed on to cultures like the Egyptians, who worked to stabilize Earth's planetary crystalline field.

Both the Earth and human bodies, as well as our DNA, are made of crystalline structures. Crystals act as record keepers of the collective consciousness of all planetary species, storing the imprints of our evolutionary journey across time. They hold the "Diamond Sun" instruction sets, which guide planetary evolution and human ascension, connecting us to the Creator.

Each crystal species has its own unique frequency and metaphysical properties, which influence how they function. Crystals are formed from one of seven geometric shapes, representing expressions of the sacred creation rays from the Seven Sacred Suns. These stars, visible in the Ursa Major constellation (the Great Bear).

Crystals have specific core geometries, such as triangles, squares, hexagons, or trapezoids. There are seven crystal systems in total: triclinic, monoclinic, orthorhombic, tetragonal, trigonal, hexagonal, and cubic. Each shape has a unique function that connects to the geometric patterns in the Earth's energy grid.

A crystal family is determined by its lattice structure, which is formed by combining different crystal systems with assigned space groups. The shape of the lattice not only defines the crystal system but also determines its physical properties and appearance.

Guardians mention that some crystal properties are greatly enhanced when in spherical shapes for concentrated effects, but raw and naked crystal formations are the best choice whenever possible. The center heart of the crystal consists of tiny rotating particles vibrating at a certain frequency which gives the crystal its unique energy. Whatever geometric form they take their crystalline structure can accrete, hold, conserve, focus or emit a range of electromagnetic frequencies from the ray system for spiritual healing, energy balancing and consciousness expansion.

CRYSTAL GRIDS:

Building a crystal grid can be a powerful way to amplify your intentions and focus energy for specific purposes, such as healing, manifestation, or protection. Here's a simple step-by-step guide to creating your own crystal grid:

1. Set Your Intention - Clarify your purpose: Before starting, decide what you want to achieve with your crystal grid (e.g., healing, abundance, protection). Either state it out loud or write it down.

2. Choose Your Location - Find a peaceful space: Choose a quiet, clean, and undisturbed area to set up your grid. Clear the space: Make sure the area is clear of clutter.

3. Select Your Crystals - Choose crystals that align with your intention. You can use a variety of crystals depending on your goal:

- Healing: Amethyst, Rose Quartz, Clear Quartz.
- Protection: Black Tourmaline, Hematite, Obsidian.
- Abundance: Citrine, Green Aventurine, Pyrite.
- Love: Rose Quartz, Rhodonite, Carnelian.

Make sure to include a central crystal (often Clear Quartz or another stone of high energy) as the focal point of your grid, which amplifies the energy of the other crystals.

Many often enjoy exploring the metaphysical uses of crystals. There's a wealth of information available, including details about geological and rock formations around the world.

4. Prepare the Crystals
- Cleanse your crystals
- Program your crystals: Hold each crystal and focus on your intention. You can mentally or verbally ask the crystal to support the goal of your grid.

5. Create the Grid Pattern
- Choose a pattern: Crystal grids are usually arranged in sacred geometry patterns, like a Flower of Life, Star of David, or a simple geometric shape like a square or circle.
- Start with the center: Place your central crystal in the middle of the grid.
- Add surrounding crystals: Begin placing your other crystals around the central stone in the pattern you've chosen. You can place them in a spiral, circle, or any layout that feels right for you.

6. Activate the Grid
- Activate with intention: Once all crystals are placed, activate the grid by focusing on your intention and channeling energy into the crystals. You can use your hands, a wand, or a smaller crystal to connect the stones.
- Visualize energy flowing: Imagine a light or energy flowing from the central crystal out to the others, forming a web of energy that connects the stones.

7. Leave the Grid in Place
- Let the grid work: Once your grid is set up and activated, leave it in place for as long as you feel necessary (days, weeks, or months depending on your intention).
- Check in with the grid: You can check in with the grid periodically to see how it feels or make adjustments if necessary.

8. Closing the Grid - Thank the crystals: When you feel your work is complete, express gratitude to the crystals for their help.
- Disassemble if desired: You can take apart the grid once you feel your intention has been fulfilled.

GRIDWORKERS

Serious crystal grid builders work with the energies of crystals, arranging them in specific patterns to enhance certain qualities, like healing, peace, prosperity, or protection.

I thoroughly enjoy building grid in my greenhouse when it's too cold for plants. The crystals seem to enjoy it too and my grids are not disturbed until I remove them.

I sometimes place feathers and flowers in my grids as well. I also love placing my crystals in my windowsills all year round.

Final Tips for Caring for Your Crystals

- **Set an Intention:** Before using your cleansed crystals, hold them in your hands, close your eyes, and set an intention. This can amplify their energy.
- **Regular Cleansing:** Cleanse your crystals regularly, especially if you use them for healing, meditation, or if they've been handled by many people.
- **Storage:** Keep your crystals in a safe, clean place, like a pouch or box, to prevent them from absorbing stray energy.

By taking the time to cleanse and recharge your crystals, you'll ensure they stay energetically vibrant and ready to support your journey.

SELF-CARE:
Inexpensive but effective

Self-care can look different for everyone, as it involves taking intentional actions to maintain and improve one's physical, mental, and emotional well-being. It's about finding what nurtures and restores you. Here are some examples of what self-care might look like:

Physical Self-Care:
- **Exercise:** Engaging in regular physical activity, like walking, yoga, or dancing.
- **Sleep:** Ensuring you get enough rest, aiming for 7-9 hours of quality sleep.
- **Nutrition:** Eating nourishing foods that fuel your body and make you feel good.
- **Relaxation:** Taking time for baths, massages, or deep breathing exercises.
- **Hydration:** Drinking enough water throughout the day.

* My favorite is taking an extra-long bath with lavender and rose quartz.

Emotional Self-Care:
- **Journaling:** Writing down your thoughts or feelings as a way to process emotions.
- **Setting Boundaries:** Saying no when you need to protect your time or energy.
- **Mindfulness and Meditation:** Practicing presence to calm your mind and manage stress. (Grounding)

Mental Self-Care:
- **Reading or Learning:** Engaging with materials that stimulate your mind or bring you joy.
- **Creative Expression:** Drawing, painting, writing, or engaging in any form of creativity.
- **Unplugging:** Taking breaks from screens and social media to recharge mentally.

Spiritual Self-Care:
- **Prayer or Meditation:** Practices that connect you to your deeper sense of meaning or spirituality.
- **Spending Time in Nature**: Taking walks outside or just sitting in natural surroundings to ground yourself.

I enjoy walking around my farm and smelling the flowers. Sweet peas, lavender, lilacs in the Spring. This also stimulates your clair for smell known as Clairalience (also sometimes referred to as clairaliency). It refers to the intuitive ability to perceive scents or odors that are not physically present, often in a psychic or spiritual context. This can involve smelling fragrances, flowers, perfumes, or other scents that might be associated with spirits, energies, or specific memories.

People who experience clairalience may smell familiar scents that seem to come from nowhere or detect unusual smells in certain situations, which could be interpreted as messages or signs.

- Ultimately, self-care is about listening to your needs and doing what makes you feel restored, balanced, and connected to yourself. It's a practice that should feel personal, not a set of rules, and it can change depending on your circumstances and needs at any given time.

- What activities make me feel truly relaxed and at peace?

- What is one small change I can make in my daily routine to take better care of myself?

- What are my favorite self-care rituals, and how can I incorporate them more often? This is KEY!!

Start a self-care ritual. I had to start one because I'm always caring for the animals and beings on my farm, I'm worn out when it came to me.

Self-Care Rituals
Focus on your breath and set a positive intention for the day. *I set my intentions before going to bed for the following day.*

Enhancement:
- Use essential oils like lavender or citrus to awaken your senses.

I love picking lavender from my garden and fresh zinnias of all colors and placing them in the house. I sometimes wonder into the back field and gather a bouquet of purple violets and bring them in the house. This helps my crown chakra and balancing for my higher morphogenetic chakras.

Sacred Bathing Ritual:
- Draw a warm bath and add Epsom salts, a few drops of essential oils (like eucalyptus or rose), and a handful of fresh herbs (such as rosemary or lavender).
- Play soothing frequency music, dim the lights, and soak to release tension.
- Visualize stress leaving your body as you relax. Place a few crystals (like Rose Quartz or Amethyst) around the tub for added energy.

Tea Meditation
Brew a cup of herbal tea (chamomile, peppermint, or green tea). As you drink, focus on the warmth, taste, and aroma, allowing it to ground you in the present moment. Use this time to express gratitude for the small joys in life.

Journaling & Reflection
Dedicate 10-15 minutes before bed to journal about your day. Write down three things you're grateful for, along with any thoughts or feelings you want to release.

- Keep a beautiful notebook and pen on your bedside table to encourage this habit. Keep track of your dreams / meditations.

Gentle Movement & Stretching
- Spend 10-15 minutes stretching or practicing yoga, focusing on areas where you hold tension. This can be especially soothing before bedtime.
- Walk your dog or just yourself along a beautiful, flowing stream and watch the currents.
- Alternative: Try a slow, mindful walk in nature, paying attention to the sights, sounds, and smells around you.

Digital Detox - Set aside one evening a week to disconnect from all screens. Use this time to reconnect with yourself by doing something creative, relaxing or just rest.

- How can I set better boundaries to protect my energy and well-being?
- What is something I need to let go of to feel more at ease?

Creative Expression Time - Dedicate time to a creative hobby that brings you joy—whether it's painting, playing music, crafting, or cooking. Let go of perfection and enjoy the process.

- Tip: Play your favorite music or light incense to set a creative mood.

Nourishing Your Inner Child - Spend an afternoon doing something you loved as a child—like coloring, picking a bouquet of flowers, climbing a tree, or building a fort out of blankets.

Healing your inner child is crucial to expanding your consciousness and opening up your higher morphogenetic chakras. But this all happens one step at a time. There are no fast tracks.

- Allow yourself to feel carefree and playful.

Journal Prompts for Self-Care and Reflection
- How am I feeling physically, emotionally, and mentally right now?
- What are three things I can do this week to show myself love?
- What activities make me feel truly relaxed and at peace?
- What is one small change I can make in my daily routine to take better care of myself?
- What am I most grateful for at this moment?
- How can I set better boundaries to protect my energy and well-being?
- What is something I need to let go of to feel more at ease?
- If I were taking care of myself as if I were someone I love, what would I do differently?
- What are my favorite self-care rituals, and how can I incorporate them more often?
- What is one kind thing I can say to myself right now?

Quick Self-Care Practices for Busy Days
- **Breathe Deeply:** Pause for a few moments to take five slow, deep breaths. This helps calm your mind and reduce stress.
- **Gratitude Check**: Write down three things you're grateful for—right now, in this moment.
- **Hydrate:** Drink a large glass of water and take a few moments to feel refreshed.
- **Stretch Break:** Stand up, stretch your arms, and roll your shoulders to release tension.

These rituals and prompts are designed to help you slow down, reconnect with yourself, and find moments of peace, even in a busy world.

Self-care is the hardest for me to prioritize. With a large farm and animals that depend entirely on me, I often find myself being the last one to be taken care of. Then by the time everyone is tended to, I'm to exhausted to tend to myself.

A key part of self-care, though, is **forgiveness.** Holding onto resentment and unforgiveness weighs heavily on your heart and mind, blocking growth and healing. Letting go of those burdens is **essential** not just for your peace of mind, but for your overall well-being and personal growth.

I used this meditation to work through unforgiveness and move beyond the victim mindset.
- I visualized all the people who had caused me pain standing around me as little children. In this meditation, I saw them as innocent, vulnerable beings, unaware of the harm they had caused.
- These children did not intend to hurt me—they were simply doing the best they could with the knowledge and emotional capacity they had at the time.
- By seeing them this way, I was able to release the resentment and offer forgiveness, freeing myself from the weight of the past. It allowed me to heal and create space for my own growth.
- *I began growing my wings!*

Water Alchemy

- Water Alchemy Infusion Meditation is a transformative practice that draws upon the belief that water holds memories and energetic imprints. It helps facilitate healing by using water's ability to absorb, transform, and release energies.

- Whether for emotional, mental, or physical well-being, this meditation encourages individuals to connect with the essence of water, allowing it to support their healing journey. Through mindful intention and visualization, water becomes a medium for transformation, providing a powerful tool for personal growth.

How Water Alchemy Infusion Meditation is Practiced:

- **Setting an Intention:** Before beginning the meditation, you set a specific intention, such as healing, emotional balance, or releasing negative energy. This helps focus your mind on the specific goal you wish to achieve.
    - **Example**: I infuse my water to activate my CRYSTALLINE LIGHT BODY.

- **Infusing the Water:** You may prepare water by placing it in a glass or container and mentally programming it with your desired intention. Some people will even speak positive affirmations to the water or hold it in their hands to transfer energy. In some practices, crystals, herbs, or essential oils may be added to the water to enhance its energy.

- **Visualization:** During the meditation, you may visualize the water's healing properties, imagining it absorbing negative emotions or energies and transforming them into positive, healing light. Visualizing the water as a source of cleansing and renewal can be powerful for emotional healing.

- **Drinking the Infused Water or Bathing in It**: After the meditation, drinking the infused water or bathing in it can help internalize the positive energy that was infused during the meditation. It is believed that the water carries the energy of your intention and healing, helping to integrate the work.

** *I infuse my bath water with Lavender and rose quartz crystals and make it into a self-care event.*

PHYSIC SELF-DEFENSE:

Many things can weaken our health by affecting our energy field or aura. However, by becoming more self-aware and practicing basic spiritual protection, we can strengthen our aura or Lightbody. This helps bring balance and improve our health on all levels, supporting our overall well-being.

- Negative emotions & destructive thoughtforms.
- Unresolved emotional or psychological conflicts, destructive relationships.
- Pharmaceuticals, drugs, alcohol, addiction, and consuming recreational substances.
- Surgery, hospitalization, and cutting into the body.
- Low EMF fields generated from technology (cellphones, computers, TV).
- Solar flares and strong magnetic field shifts, EMF fluctuations.
- Accidents or events that cause physical stress, shocks, or emotionally traumatic experiences.
- International air travel, traveling to areas with different grid systems or hemispheres.
- Extreme grief, depression, guilt, shame, or loneliness.

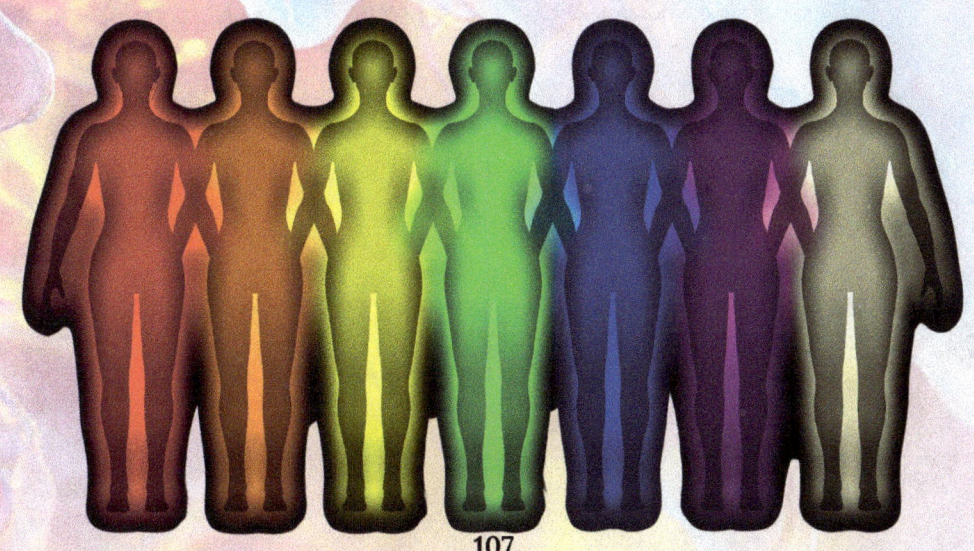

Understanding Auric Colors and Their Meanings

Your aura is an energetic field that surrounds your body, reflecting your physical, emotional, mental, and spiritual state. Auras can appear in different colors, which can change based on your mood, health, thoughts, and experiences. Here's a guide to understanding the various auric colors and what they might reveal about you.

1. **Red Aura**
   - **Meaning:** Vitality, passion, strength, and energy
   - **Positive Aspects:** Indicates high energy, strong willpower, confidence, and determination. Often seen in people who are driven and take action.
   - **Negative Aspects:** Can signal anger, frustration, or a tendency toward impulsiveness. It may also indicate stress or tension if it appears muddy or dark.

REMEDIES:
- Grounding
- Breathing Exercises
- Energy Clearing
- Self-Reflection & Emotional Release
- Meditation & Mindfulness
- Self-Care

2. **Orange Aura**
   - **Meaning:** Creativity, joy, emotional health, and sociability.
   - **Positive Aspects:** Represents joy, creativity, warmth, and openness. Seen in people who are outgoing, adventurous, and enjoy social interactions.
   - **Negative Aspects:** Can suggest overindulgence, addiction, or a lack of emotional balance if it appears murky.

3. **Yellow Aura**
   - **Meaning:** Optimism, intellect, confidence, and personal power.
   - **Positive Aspects**: Reflects a positive outlook, mental clarity, and intellectual curiosity. Often seen in people who are cheerful, confident, and optimistic.
   - **Negative Aspects:** If muddy, it can indicate overthinking, anxiety, or fear of failure.

4. Green Aura
- **Meaning**: Balance, healing, compassion, and growth.
- **Positive Aspects:** Represents healing energy, compassion, love, and a connection to nature. Common in people who are nurturing and empathetic.
- **Negative Aspects:** If dark or dull, it may indicate jealousy, resentment, or an inability to forgive.

5. Blue Aura
- **Meaning**: Communication, peace, truth, and clarity.
- **Positive Aspects**: Reflects calmness, sincerity, and effective communication. Seen in those who are intuitive, truthful, and expressive.
- **Negative Aspects:** If dark or muddy, it can suggest suppressed feelings, fear of speaking up, or difficulty in expressing emotions.

6. **Indigo Aura**
   - **Meaning:** Intuition, spiritual awareness, wisdom, and insight.
   - **Positive Aspects:** Represents deep intuition, psychic abilities, and spiritual awareness. Often found in individuals who are introspective and highly intuitive.
   - **Negative Aspects:** A murky indigo aura may indicate fear of the unknown or confusion about one's life path.

7. **Violet or Purple Aura**
   - **Meaning:** Spiritual connection, enlightenment, and higher consciousness.
   - **Positive Aspects:** Indicates spiritual awareness, a deep connection to the divine, and a sense of purpose. Common in those who are on a spiritual journey or have psychic abilities.
   - **Negative Aspects:** If it appears muddy or dark, it may signal disconnection from one's spiritual path or feelings of isolation.

8. Pink Aura
- **Meaning**: Love, kindness, compassion, and gentleness
- **Positive Aspects**: Reflects love, kindness, selflessness, and compassion. Often seen in those who are generous, caring, and have a nurturing spirit.
- **Negative Aspects**: If murky, it can indicate issues with self-love or feelings of being taken advantage of.
- **Related Chakra**: Often associated with the Heart Chakra but also linked to higher spiritual love.

9. White or Silver Aura
- **Meaning**: Purity, protection, spiritual connection, and clarity.
- **Positive Aspects**: Indicates purity, spiritual awakening, and protection. Seen in people who are spiritually advanced or have a strong connection to their higher self.
- **Negative Aspects**: A dull or grayish-white aura can indicate exhaustion or a loss of vitality.

10. Gold Aura
- **Meaning:** Divine protection, wisdom, enlightenment, and abundance.
- **Positive Aspects:** Reflects spiritual enlightenment, abundance, and protection. Often seen in individuals who are spiritually enlightened or leaders.
- **Negative Aspects:** Rarely negative, but a tarnished or dim gold aura can suggest arrogance or feeling disconnected from spiritual roots.

11. Black Aura
- **Meaning:** Protection, hidden emotions, or blockages.
- **Positive Aspects:** Black can sometimes appear in the aura of those who are protective of themselves or others.
- **Negative Aspects:** Often indicates blockages, unresolved trauma, or negative attachments. It can also signify a heavy or depressed state.
- **Related Chakra:** indicates an area that needs healing.

12. Gray Aura
- **Meaning**: Uncertainty, confusion, or stuck energy.
- **Positive Aspects:** Can represent a person in transition, exploring new paths.
- **Negative Aspects:** Often signals indecisiveness, confusion, or unresolved issues. It can also indicate that someone is feeling drained or uninspired.
- **Usually looks foggy**

Understanding Auric Colors in Context
- **Vibrant Colors**: Indicate a healthy and balanced energy field.
- **Dark or Murky Colors:** Suggest blockages, stress, or emotional challenges.
- **Shifting Colors:** Your aura may change colors throughout the day depending on your mood, environment, or interactions with others.

How to Observe and Interpret Your Aura
- **Meditation:** Close your eyes, take deep breaths, and visualize your energy field. What colors come to mind?
- **Mirror Technique:** Stand in front of a mirror with a white background, soften your gaze, and focus on the space around your head and shoulders.
- **Energy Sensitivity:** Pay attention to how you feel around certain people or environments. Your aura can react, and shift based on external influences.

By understanding your auric colors, you can gain insights into your current state and focus on practices to enhance your well-being.

Common Colors You Might See and Their Meanings

- **Red:** Vitality, strength, passion, but also anger or stress.
- **Orange:** Creativity, joy, emotional warmth, or social energy.
- **Yellow:** Confidence, intellect, optimism, or overthinking.
- **Green:** Healing, compassion, balance, or growth.
- **Blue**: Communication, calm, sincerity, or truth.
- **Indigo:** Intuition, insight, or spiritual awareness.
- **Purple/Violet:** Spiritual connection, enlightenment, or psychic abilities.
- **White:** Purity, protection, high spiritual connection.
- **Gray or Black Spots:** These can indicate blockages, unresolved emotions, or physical ailments.

How to See Other People's Auras
- Seeing auras is a skill that can be developed with patience, practice, and mindfulness. Although some people may be naturally attuned to seeing auras, anyone can learn to perceive the subtle energy fields surrounding others with time and dedication. Here's a step-by-step guide to help you start seeing auras.

Start Practicing on Your Own Hand

1. Hold your hand up against a light-colored background.
2. Relax your gaze and look at the space just above or around your hand, not directly at it.
3. Focus on the area where your fingers meet the background. You might start to notice a faint glow or outline around your hand—this is the beginning of perceiving the aura.
4. With time and practice, you may begin to see colors or patterns.

Techniques to Enhance Your Aura Vision

- **Peripheral Vision:** Your peripheral vision is more sensitive to subtle energies. Try looking slightly off to the side of the person instead of directly at them.
- **Blink Slowly:** If your eyes get tired, blink slowly and refocus. Sometimes, a moment of rest can help you perceive the aura more clearly when you look again.
- **Practice in Nature:** Try observing the aura of trees, plants, or animals. Nature's energy fields are often easier to perceive and can help train your eyes.
- **Meditation & Visualization:** Spend time meditating on your third eye and visualizing energy fields. This can sharpen your intuition and enhance your ability to see auras.
- **Crystal Support:** Using crystals like Amethyst, Lapis Lazuli, or Selenite can help enhance your intuitive abilities. Hold one while practicing aura reading.

How to Interpret What You See

- **Observe Patterns:** Take note of the colors, intensity, and shape of the aura. A vibrant, bright aura indicates good health and a positive mindset, while a dull or murky aura may suggest stress or emotional turmoil.
- **Check for Shifts**: Auras can change depending on a person's emotions, health, and energy levels. The colors you see may shift if the person is going through different experiences or emotions.
- **Trust Your Intuition**: Sometimes, you may get a feeling or insight about the person's energy that goes beyond what you see. Trust these intuitive impressions.

By developing the ability to see auras, you can gain a deeper understanding of the energies around you and improve your connection with yourself and others. Keep practicing, stay open-minded, and remember to trust your intuition.

How to Clear Your Auric Field & Signs It Needs Clearing

Your auric field, or aura, is an energetic shield that surrounds your body. It helps protect your physical, emotional, and spiritual well-being by interacting with the energies around you.

Signs Your Auric Field Needs Clearing

- Feeling Drained or Fatigued
    - If you often feel tired or lethargic, even after a good night's sleep, it could be a sign that your aura is weighed down by stagnant energy.
- Mood Swings or Emotional Overwhelm
    - Sudden feelings of sadness, anxiety, or irritability, especially when they seem to come out of nowhere, can indicate your auric field has absorbed negative energies.
- Difficulty Focusing or Mental Fog
    - An unclear aura can affect your mental clarity, making it harder to concentrate, remember things, or make decisions.
- Frequent Negative Thoughts
    - If you notice an increase in negative self-talk, pessimism, or feeling stuck in a loop of unproductive thoughts, your aura might be cluttered.
- Physical Symptoms Without Medical Explanation
    - Headaches, muscle tension, or unexplained aches and pains can sometimes be a sign that your energy field is out of balance.
- If you feel drained after being in certain environments or around specific people, your aura may be affected by external energies.
- A cloudy aura can block inspiration, leaving you feeling stuck or unmotivated.

How to Clear Your Auric Field

Smudging with Sage or Palo Santo
- Light a bundle of sage or a stick of Palo Santo and allow the smoke to envelop your body. Slowly move the smoke from the top of your head to your feet, focusing on areas where you feel tension.
- As you do this, set an intention like: "I release any negative energy and welcome peace and light into my aura."
- *Tip: Make sure you open a window to allow the negative energy to leave your space.*

Salt Bath Soak
- Fill a bathtub with warm water and add a cup of sea salt or Epsom salt. Soak for at least 20 minutes to cleanse and recharge your aura.
- You can also include a few drops of essential oils like lavender or eucalyptus.
- If you don't have access to a bathtub, a salt scrub in the shower can also be effective.

Crystal Healing
- Crystals like Clear Quartz, Selenite, Amethyst, and Black Tourmaline are excellent for clearing and protecting your auric field.
- Hold a crystal in your hand or place it on your body during meditation to draw out negative energies.
- You can also use a Selenite wand to "scan" your aura by slowly moving it from head to toe, visualizing it absorbing any negativity.

Energy Sweeping with Your Hands
- Rub your hands together to generate warmth, then slowly move your hands around your body, as if you're brushing away invisible dust.
- Visualize any negative energy being swept away and dissolved into the Earth.
- This technique is especially helpful if you're feeling heavy or drained after interacting with others.

Visualization & Meditation
- Sit quietly, close your eyes, and take deep breaths. Visualize a bright, white light surrounding your body, filling your aura with cleansing energy.
- Imagine this light dissolving any dark spots or stagnant energy, leaving you feeling refreshed and vibrant.
- You can also visualize yourself standing under a waterfall of golden light that washes away any negativity.

Nature Therapy
- Spending time in nature can naturally cleanse your auric field. Walk barefoot on grass (grounding), sit by a tree, or visit a park to connect with Earth's natural energy.
- Let the wind, sun, or water cleanse your aura by visualizing it sweeping away any negativity.

Additional Tips for Maintaining a Clear Aura

- **Set Boundaries:** Protect your energy by setting boundaries with people or environments that drain you.
- **Practice Gratitude:** Regular gratitude journaling.
- **Regular Self-Care.**
- **Carry Protective Crystals**: Keep a piece of Black Tourmaline, Obsidian, or Labradorite with you for protection against negative energies.

By regularly clearing your auric field, you'll feel lighter, more energized, and better able to handle whatever life throws your way.

GUARD YOUR ENERGY!!

HEALING FREQUENCIES:

Frequency: The rate at which sound waves vibrate. It is measured in hertz (Hz), which indicates the number of cycles per second.

By integrating healing frequencies into your wellness practices, you can enhance your mental, emotional, and physical well-being, helping you achieve a state of balance and harmony.

The Science Behind Healing Frequencies

- **Brainwave Entrainment:** Certain frequencies can influence the brain's electrical activity, helping to shift your brainwaves into a more relaxed or focused state. For example, listening to 432 Hz can help induce alpha brainwaves, associated with deep relaxation.
    - In 1953 the music industry shifted the standard tuning frequency from 432 Hz to 440 Hz.

- **Resonance:** The concept that every object, including your body and cells, has its own natural frequency. Healing frequencies work by resonating with these natural frequencies to promote balance.

- **Vibration and Cells:** Research has shown that sound vibrations can influence cellular function. For example, specific frequencies can help reduce inflammation, stimulate the immune system, or improve emotional well-being.

Each sound wave vibrates at a specific frequency, measured in hertz (Hz), and different frequencies can have unique effects on our mind, body, and spirit. Let's explore the concept of healing frequencies, their benefits, and how they can be used to promote well-being.

The 9 Solfeggio Frequencies

- Natural Anesthetic
- Heals Physical Pain
- Heals Emotional Pain
- Increases Courage
- Cleanses Aura
- Emotional Wellness

- Rejuvenates
- Regenerates Tissues
- Heals Internal Organs
- Increases Energy
- Immune System
- Heals Auric Field

- Liberates Guilt & Fear
- Turns Grief Into Joy
- Cleanses Negativity
- Empowers Goals
- Inner Peace
- Root Chakra

- Facilitates Change
- Enhances Creativity
- Clears Negative Energy
- Manifests Intentions
- Cleanses Trauma
- Sacral Chakra

- Love Frequency
- Transformational
- Divine Miracles
- Self Confidence
- Restores DNA
- Solar Plexus Chakra

- Attracts Love
- Positive Energy
- Balances Emotions
- Heals Relationships
- Brings Harmony
- Heart Chakra

- Self Expression
- Problem Solving
- Cleanses Cells
- Cleanses Viral Infections
- Purifies Body & Mind
- Throat Chakra

- Return To Spiritual Order
- Awakens Intuition
- Raises Cell Vibrations
- Awakens Inner Strength
- Bridge To Higher Self
- Third Eye Chakra

- Christ Consiousness
- Pure Miracle Tone
- High Level Intuition
- Telepathy
- Psychic Vision
- Crown Chakra

Ancient Healing Tones

Tips for Maximizing the Benefits
Be Mindful of Volume: Healing frequencies don't need to be loud to be effective. Keep the volume at a comfortable level. Listen with an Open Mind: Approach the experience with openness and curiosity. The more you relax and trust the process, the more effective it can be.

- 432 Hz is believed to be in tune with the natural frequencies of nature, and when heard in conjunction with the ocean, it can restore a sense of balance and alignment in the body, promoting overall well-being.
- **Nature Immersion:** Spend time in environments where these natural frequencies occur, such as forests, oceans, or near rivers to absorb healing vibrations.

12D SHIELD PROTECTION:

The **12th Dimensional Light Shield** is a powerful way to strengthen your lightbody and protect your aura from negative or heavy energies.

- The 12th Dimensional Shield strengthens our aura by reconnecting us to our 12th-dimensional blueprint, or Krystal body. This practice helps us set energetic boundaries, allowing us to protect ourselves from uninvited, discordant energies.

- It also supports physical and energetic health by bringing balance to our body and restoring communication with our spiritual guides and star family. As we work with the 12D shield, we reconnect with the wisdom of our true origins, which may lead us to understand light language or uncover hidden knowledge about our planet and our history.

- We use the six-pointed star, or merkabah, to represent this process. While many are familiar with this practice, let's now go through the steps for those new to the 12D shield.

THIS IS THE 12D PROCESS

- Visualize a silver six-pointed star, the Star of David, in the center of your brain. This symbol represents unity and oneness with God. Feel that unity as the star moves down through your body, along your chakra column, and releases between your legs.

- Send the merkabah star all the way to the core of the Earth. Imagine a huge merkabah star at the planet's center, filled with your love and intention, bringing unity to the Earth and all beings on it.

See EnergeticSynthesis.com - Lisa Renee
YouTube: 12D Shield Building Technique

- Visualize a stream of platinum energy surrounding you from the Earth's core. As you breathe in, you may feel a cool, menthol-like sensation, similar to eucalyptus. This represents your connection to the God force: I am God, I am Sovereign, I am Free. This is your true Krystal origin.

- With each breath, connect to the six-pointed star at the Earth's core and draw it up. When it returns, let it stop about 12 inches below your feet. This area holds the core signature of your Krystal body, linking to your aura.

- Visualize the six-pointed star 12 inches below your feet, and watch as a circular platform forms beneath you. This platform is your shield and the foundation of your spiritual house. See it growing firm and supportive, with the star at the center as your core, pillar, and strength—it belongs to you alone, a protection from God.

- As you feel the strength of your foundation, imagine a platinum energy radiating from it, forming a circular pillar of white light around you. This light surrounds your body, every cell, and every part of your energy system, connecting you to the crystalline light of God. It protects and supports you, providing a solid foundation and security.

- Visualize the pillar of light building over your legs, hips, waist, and shoulders, and then extending above your head. Strengthen this pillar to about 3-4 feet above your head. This is the first step in creating a protective shield for your aura.

- By using this technique, you can test and protect the boundaries of your energy field, allowing only invited energies to enter. This helps you learn to set boundaries and stabilize your own energy before sharing it with others or the planet. This process is called "commanding your personal space."

- Visualize your platinum shield building around you, covering your body from about 12 inches below your feet to 3-4 feet above your head, fully protecting your aura with a strong pillar of light.

- Create a similar foundation at the top. Connect with the six-pointed star at the base of your spiritual house, then bring it up through your body's center.

- The six-pointed star represents unity of the inner masculine and feminine energies. As it moves up, see it reach the crown chakra and extend 3-4 feet above your head. Let the thick white light grow stronger in your core, forming your central vertical channel, or monadic staff, which supports your chakras.

- If you cannot see this, just intend it for that is enough. In your vision, as you intend to put the six-pointed star 3 and half or 4 feet above your head see it start to build. It will start in its own movement of spinning to start to build yet another circular foundation above your head. You are protected below, and you are protected above. As you create another lid to seal yourself inside your personal pillar of light, this is the roof of your house, the roof of your spiritual body.

- We are going to see that "lid" as a circular platform just like you did below on your foundation. Create a circular roof that is like your lid on top of your shield. And as you feel that roof firmly being built these are the spiritual energies of your inner god force. Seal that seal in to the top of your platinum pillar of light. When this happens it almost feels like a hermetic seal as you are fully suspended in this protective light, fully shielded in your spiritual house and from this place you can use discernment, you can boundary test in all modalities and all decision and in all things that cross your path.

- If something becomes unclear or confused, allow it to be tested against your shield. Is it of your resonance? Is it not of your resonance? If it is not, do not fear it, let it go and move on your personal path. You are not missing anything. You didn't make a bad decision. There is no mistake, only that which resonates with your personal heart-based God force and that which does not.

- So you again feel yourself suspended in the protective spiritual house and pillar of God's light. Program it through I am God, I am Sovereign, I am Free and allow nothing that is not aligned with those frequencies to enter your field, to enter your shield.

- Focus on the six-pointed star, your Unity Merkaba, 3-4 feet above your head. Now, send the star into deep space, connecting it with the Heart of the Universe, the heart of God. See it travel through a platinum energy line from the top of your shield to the core of the Cosmic Heart.

- From this place, invite your Higher Self, God Self, and Ascension Guides, those aligned with your highest evolution, to join you. Know that you are supported and never alone, always connected to your spiritual family.

- Thank your Ascension guides and God, allowing yourself to feel peace, balance, and harmony. Trust that you are on the path of Ascension and will receive what you need when the time is right. Let go of all worries and doubts, surrendering them to God. In love and gratitude, complete your meditation and seal your intention.

- If something becomes unclear or confused, allow it to be tested against your shield. **Is it of your resonance? Is it not of your resonance?** If it is not, do not fear it, let it go and move on your personal path. You are not missing anything. You didn't make a bad decision. There is no mistake, only that which resonates with your personal heart-based God force and that which does not.

- Feel yourself suspended in the protective spiritual house and pillar of God's light. Program it through I am God, I am Sovereign, I am Free and allow nothing that is not aligned with those frequencies to enter your field, to enter your shield.

- Focus on the six-pointed star, your Unity Merkaba, 3-4 feet above your head. Now, send the star into deep space, connecting it with the Heart of the Universe, the heart of God. See it travel through a platinum energy line from the top of your shield to the core of the Cosmic Heart.

- From this place, invite your Higher Self, God Self, and Ascension Guides, those aligned with your highest evolution, to join you. Know that you are supported and never alone, always connected to your spiritual family.

- Thank your Ascension guides and God, allowing yourself to feel peace, balance, and harmony. Trust that you are on the path of Ascension and will receive what you need when the time is right. Let go of all worries and doubts, surrendering them to God. In love and gratitude, complete your meditation and seal your intention.

I use the 12D shield daily and test the boundaries of all spirits.
- *The astral realm is chaotic and unsafe right now, which is why there's so much misinformation on social media due to infiltration.*

- *If you don't control your mind, something else will.*

SPIRIT GUIIDES

What Are Spirit Guides?
- **Spiritual Allies**: Spirit guides are believed to be spiritual beings who exist on a higher plane of consciousness. They are here to help us navigate life's challenges, provide insights, and encourage personal and spiritual growth.
- **Non-Physical Beings**: They are not limited by the physical realm and can communicate with us through signs, symbols, intuition, dreams, or even feelings.
- **Assigned from Birth**: Some spirit guides are said to be with us from birth, while others may come and go depending on our life circumstances, lessons, or needs.

Spirit Guide Concepts: Understanding and Connecting with Your Spiritual Guides

- If you are reading this, you have an ASCENSION TEAM ASSIGNED SPECIFICALLY TO YOU.
- Let's explore the key concepts behind spirit guides, the different types of guides, how they interact with us, and how to connect with them.

1. Guardian Angels
- Guardian angels are protective guides assigned to you from birth. They keep you safe, protect your energy, and offer unconditional love and support.
- They may step in during dangerous situations or when you need extra protection, offering comfort and a sense of safety.

2. Ancestors and Ancestral Guides
- These guides are often deceased relatives who watch over you and offer guidance from the spirit world. They have a deep connection to your lineage and can help with family-related issues or generational healing.
- They may offer insights related to family patterns, traditions, and inherited strengths.

3. Animal Spirit Guides (Totems)
- Animal guides, or spirit animals, represent certain qualities or skills that you may need to develop or embrace. They can appear in your life as animals you encounter frequently or in dreams.
- They bring messages related to instinct, courage, strength, or other qualities associated with their species.

4. How Spirit Guides Communicate with Us
- **Intuition:** A sudden knowing or gut feeling is often a nudge from your guides.
- **Signs and Symbols:** Repeated numbers, feathers, coins, or other meaningful symbols may be their way of sending messages.
- **Dreams:** Spirit guides can appear in your dreams, providing insights or messages while your conscious mind is relaxed. You may want to start a dream journal.
- **Synchronicities:** Unusual coincidences or serendipitous events are often orchestrated by guides to get your attention.
- **Inner Voice or Thought:** Sometimes, guides may communicate through a voice in your mind that feels different from your usual inner dialogue. [This is why 12D shielding is crucial daily].
- **Emotional or Physical Sensations:** Feeling a sudden warmth, chills, or tingles can indicate the presence of a guide.

5. Ascended Masters
- These are highly evolved spiritual beings who once lived as humans and have attained enlightenment, such as Buddha, Jesus, or Quan Yin. They offer higher wisdom and spiritual teachings.
- They assist with spiritual growth, enlightenment, and aligning with your higher purpose.

6. Spirit Helpers or Guides for Specific Areas of Life
- These guides specialize in particular areas, such as career, health, creativity, or relationships. They may come into your life temporarily to help with specific projects or challenges.
- They provide insights, creative ideas, or practical advice tailored to your current needs.

ALWAYS 12D SHIELD BEFORE ATTEMPTING TO CONNECT WITH OTHER BEINGS OR ALLOWING OTHER BEING INTO YOUR HEART SPACE

How to Connect with Your Spirit Guides
Connecting with your spirit guides is about tuning into their frequency and becoming more aware of their presence. Here's how you can build a stronger connection:

1. Meditation and Visualization
- **Meditation:** Sit quietly, focus on your breath, and invite your spirit guides to join you. Visualize a warm light surrounding you and ask your guides to reveal themselves.
- **Visualization Exercise:** Picture yourself in a beautiful, peaceful place. Invite your guides to meet you there and ask any questions you have.

2. Journaling and Automatic Writing
- **Automatic Writing**: Set an intention to communicate with your guides, then write down whatever comes to mind without overthinking. Let your pen flow freely.
- **Journaling Prompts**: Ask questions like, "What do my spirit guides want me to know today?" and write down any thoughts or impressions that arise.

3. Pay Attention to Signs
- **Be Open**: Once you invite your guides into your life, be open to noticing signs and synchronicities. Keep a journal of any recurring symbols, numbers, or meaningful events.
- **Ask for Confirmation**: If you receive a sign but are unsure of its meaning, ask your guides for clarification. They often respond with another sign.

4. Use Tools for Divination
- **Tarot or Oracle Cards**: Use these tools to receive messages from your guides. Set the intention that your reading is guided by your spirit team.

*Being steeped in religion for over 40 years, I was programmed to fear Tarot and spiritual cards. Now, I have about six decks and use them regularly for confirmation.

5. Building a Relationship with Your Guides
- **Show Gratitude**: Thank your guides regularly for their help and guidance, even if you're unsure if you're receiving it. Gratitude strengthens your connection.
- **Trust Your Intuition**: Trust the messages you receive, even if they don't make immediate sense. Over time, you'll become more confident in recognizing their guidance.

6. Create a Sacred Space: Dedicate a corner of your home for meditation, journaling, or simply sitting quietly to connect with your guides.
- **Practice Regularly**: Like any relationship, your connection with your guides will strengthen with time and consistency. Make it a habit to check in with them regularly.

Yes, we absolutely all have guides. Ask your guides to reveal themselves to you and then open your heart to receive them.

7. Signs You've Connected with Your Spirit Guides
- You experience sudden clarity or "aha" moments.
- You feel a comforting presence during times of stress or anxiety.
- You begin to notice an increase in synchronicities and meaningful coincidences. (See next section)
- You receive guidance that turns out to be helpful or insightful.
- You feel a sense of peace, joy, or lightness after attempting to connect.

Final Thoughts: Trusting the Process
- Connecting with your spirit guides requires an open mind, patience, and trust in your own inner wisdom. The more you practice tuning into their presence, the more you'll recognize their subtle nudges and messages. Whether you're seeking guidance on a specific question or simply wish to deepen your spiritual journey, your spirit guides are always here to support you.

What Are Synchronicities?
- Synchronicities are meaningful coincidences that seem too perfectly timed to be random.
- These events or signs often feel like the universe is speaking directly to you, offering guidance, confirmation, or reassurance.
- The concept was first introduced by the famous psychologist Carl Jung, who believed that synchronicities are not just random events but rather a reflection of the interconnectedness of all things.
- While they may appear as mere coincidences, synchronicities carry a deeper significance, aligning with your thoughts, desires, or experiences in a way that feels intentional.
- These experiences can provide insight, guidance, or validation, especially during times of uncertainty or when you're seeking answers.

Examples of Synchronicities

- **Seeing Repeating Numbers:**
    - You keep noticing the numbers 11:11, 222, or 444 on clocks, license plates, or receipts. This is often interpreted as a sign from the universe, suggesting you're on the right path or encouraging you to pay attention to your thoughts.
- **Hearing a Song with a Specific Message:**
    - You're thinking about a problem, and suddenly, a song plays on the radio with lyrics that provide the answer or comfort you needed.
- **Running into the Right Person at the Right Time:**
    - You've been thinking about reaching out to an old friend, and suddenly, you bump into them on the street, or they unexpectedly call you.
- **Books or Articles Appearing at the Perfect Moment:**
    - You're grappling with a question, and a book falls off a shelf, or an article pops up online that addresses exactly what you needed to hear.

Dreams That Predict Events:
- You dream about something or someone, and the next day, it happens in real life.
- These dreams often feel more vivid or intense than usual.

Overhearing a Conversation Relevant to Your Situation:
- You're thinking about making a big life decision, and you overhear strangers discussing a similar situation with the exact advice you were looking for.

What Do Synchronicities Mean?

Synchronicities are often seen as signs from the universe, spirit guides, or your higher self, trying to communicate with you. They can be interpreted as messages that:

- **Affirm You're on the Right Path:** If you've been questioning a decision, synchronicities can serve as confirmation that you're moving in the right direction.

- **Encourage Self-Reflection:** They often prompt you to pay attention to your thoughts, feelings, or surroundings, leading to deeper self-awareness.

- **Guide You to Take Action:** If you've been procrastinating or feeling stuck, a synchronistic event may nudge you to take the next step or seize an opportunity.

- **Answer Questions You've Been Contemplating:** They may provide answers to questions you've been asking, especially when you're open and receptive to guidance.

Examples of Personal Interpretation of Synchronicities

Seeing 11:11 Repeatedly:
- Often interpreted as a sign of spiritual alignment or that your thoughts are manifesting quickly. It could be a nudge to stay positive and focused on your goals.

Dreaming of an Old Friend:
- If you dream of someone you haven't thought of in years, it might mean there's a message related to them or an aspect of your past you need to revisit or heal.

Encountering Symbols Like Feathers or Coins:
- Finding feathers, coins, or other symbols in unexpected places is often seen as a sign that you're being supported or watched over by spirit guides or loved ones who have passed.

How to Recognize and Attract Synchronicities

Be Present and Mindful:
- The more aware you are of your surroundings, the easier it is to notice synchronicities when they occur. Practice mindfulness and stay in the moment.

Set an Intention:
- Ask the universe or your spirit guides for signs. For example, you might say, "Show me a clear sign if I'm on the right path." Then, stay open to how that sign might appear.

Trust Your Intuition:
- Synchronicities often come with a gut feeling or a sense that something significant just happened. Trust that feeling rather than dismissing it as a mere coincidence.

Keep a Journal:
- Write down any synchronicities you experience. This helps you recognize patterns and see how these events are guiding you over time.

Stay Open and Receptive:
- Synchronicities tend to happen more frequently when you're open, curious, and in a state of flow. Let go of trying to control everything and allow life to unfold naturally.

Final Thoughts on Synchronicities

- Synchronicities can feel magical, bringing a sense of wonder and connection to something greater than yourself.

- They can be seen as gentle reminders that the universe is listening and responding to your energy.

- While they don't always come with a clear, immediate explanation, trust that they are guiding you towards your highest good.

- Whether you view synchronicities as messages from the divine, your higher self, or simply meaningful coincidences, they can provide comfort, insight, and inspiration on your life journey.

Receiving Guidance and Messages

- Ask Questions:
  - If you have specific questions or need clarity on something in your life, ask your guides now. Be open to receiving answers in whatever form they come—through words, symbols, or feelings.

- Express Gratitude:
  - Before concluding, thank your spirit guides for their presence and guidance. A simple "Thank you for your love, wisdom, and protection" is enough.

Angel Numbers

Angel Numbers and Their Meanings

- Angel numbers are sequences of numbers that are believed to carry spiritual messages.
- Whether seen as signs from angels, the universe, or spirit guides, these numbers are interpreted as guiding forces in various areas of life.
- While there is no scientific evidence supporting their validity, many people find personal meaning in the patterns they see, using these numbers as a tool for reflection, guidance, and affirmation.
- Angel numbers are sequences of numbers that carry divine guidance from the spiritual realm.
- Many believe that these numbers are a way for angels, spirit guides, or the universe to communicate with us, offering encouragement, support, or guidance.
- Each number has a specific meaning, and noticing these numbers repeatedly is often a sign that you're being guided or protected.

List of common angel numbers, their meanings, and how they might apply to your life.

- **Angel Number 111**
    - **Meaning:** New beginnings, manifestation, and alignment
    - **Message**: You are in alignment with your spiritual path, and your thoughts are manifesting rapidly. Be mindful of your thoughts, as they have the power to create your reality.
    - **Guidance:** Focus on positivity and set clear intentions. Now is the time to plant seeds for the future.

- **Angel Number 222**
    - **Meaning:** Balance, harmony, and partnerships
    - **Message:** Your angels are encouraging you to trust the process. Balance and patience are key right now.
    - This number often appears when you're on the right path but may need to be more patient.

- **Angel Number 333**
    - **Meaning**: Guidance, spiritual growth, and encouragement.
    - **Message**: The ascended masters and your spirit guides are with you, offering love, support, and encouragement. This is a reminder to express your truth and align with your spiritual purpose.
    - **Guidance:** Be open to receiving help from the divine. This is a sign to pursue your passions and share your gifts with the world.

- **Angel Number 444**
    - **Meaning**: Protection, stability, and building solid foundations.
    - **Message:** You are surrounded by angels who are protecting and guiding you. This number signifies that you are on the right path and that your efforts are being supported.
    - **Guidance:** Stay focused on your goals and keep moving forward. Your hard work is laying the foundation for future success.

- **Angel Number 555**
    - **Meaning**: Change, transformation, and new opportunities.
    - **Message:** A significant change is on the horizon. This change may feel sudden or unexpected, but it will lead to positive growth and new opportunities.
    - **Guidance:** Embrace change with an open mind and heart. Trust that these changes are for your highest good and are helping you grow.

- **Angel Number 666**
    - **Meaning**: Balance, reflection, and alignment with purpose.
    - **Message:** This number is often misunderstood. It's not a bad omen but rather a reminder to refocus on your spiritual and personal goals. You may have been too focused on the material world.
    - **Guidance**: Take time to reconnect with your spiritual self, practice self-care, and find balance in your life.

- **Angel Number 777**
    - **Meaning:** Spiritual awakening, luck, and divine guidance.
    - **Message:** This number is a powerful sign of divine intervention. You're on the right spiritual path, and the universe is aligning to support you. It's a confirmation that you're on the path of spiritual enlightenment.
    - **Guidance:** Continue following your intuition and spiritual practices. This is a time of deep spiritual growth and awakening.

- **Angel Number 888**
    - **Meaning:** Abundance, financial prosperity, and success.
    - **Message:** The universe is sending abundance your way. This could relate to financial success, opportunities, or personal growth. It's a sign that your hard work is paying off.
    - **Guidance:** Stay open to receiving blessings and be grateful for the abundance you already have. It's also a reminder to share your wealth and good fortune.

- **Angel Number 999**
    - **Meaning:** Completion, closure, and new beginnings.
    - **Message:** A chapter in your life is coming to an end, making way for new beginnings. This is a sign that it's time to let go of what no longer serves you.
    - **Guidance:** Release the past with gratitude and prepare to embrace a new journey. Trust that everything is aligning for your highest good.

- **Angel Number 000**
    - **Meaning**: Infinite possibilities, unity, and oneness.
    - **Message**: You are one with the universe, and your spiritual guides are reminding you of your infinite potential.
    - This number signifies the completion of a cycle and the beginning of a new one.
    - **Guidance:** Take this time to reflect, meditate, and connect with your higher self. You have limitless potential to create and manifest.

Other Notable Angel Numbers

- **1010**: Focus on spiritual development and growth. Keep a positive mindset as new opportunities arise.

- **1212**: Your thoughts are aligned with your goals. Trust that you are on the right path, and everything is working out in your favor.

- **1234**: This is a sign of progress and taking steps in the right direction. Trust in the process and keep moving forward.

- **2020**: A call to trust the divine timing of your life. You are being guided towards your soul's purpose.

- **707**: Encouragement to continue on your spiritual journey. The universe is recognizing your efforts.

Opening Your Heart and Mind Meditation
Focus on Your Heart Center:

- Bring your awareness to the center of your chest. Visualize a beautiful, glowing light (in a color that feels right to you) expanding from your heart.
- As you breathe, allow this light to grow brighter and more expansive, filling your entire being with love, peace, and openness.
- **Set Your Intention:**
    - Silently or aloud, set the intention to connect with your spirit guides:
        - "I invite my spirit guides to come forward. I am open to your wisdom, love, and guidance. Please show me what I need to know.

I always set my intentions before going to bed for that night and the next day. I never leave it to random experiences. If necessary, I bend time and extend time for the next day. Yes, it works.

How to Recognize and Interpret Angel Numbers

- **Stay Mindful and Aware:** Pay attention when you repeatedly see a specific number sequence. It might show up on license plates, receipts, clocks, or even in your dreams.

- **Tune into Your Feelings:** When you notice an angel number, take a moment to pause and reflect. What were you thinking about when you saw the number? How did it make you feel?

- **Ask for Guidance:** If you're unsure of the meaning, ask your angels for clarity. You can do this through prayer, meditation, or simply speaking your intention aloud.

- **Trust Your Intuition:** Ultimately, angel numbers are personal. Trust your intuition to interpret what the message means for you in the context of your current life circumstances.

Meeting Your Spirit Guide Team

Call Upon Your Guides Silently or aloud, say:
- "I invite my spirit guides, angels, and guardians to join me in this sacred space. Please come forward and make your presence known."

Wait Patiently and Observe:
- As you stand in your sacred space, be open to whatever comes through. You may see, hear, feel, or simply sense the presence of your guides. Each person's experience is unique.

- Your guides may appear as light beings, animals, ancestors, or just a feeling of warmth and love. Trust whatever shows up for you.

Connect and Communicate:
- You may want to ask them questions, seek guidance on an issue, or simply express gratitude for their support.

- Listen closely to any messages, impressions, or feelings that arise. You might hear words, see images, or simply get a sense of knowing.

Connecting with Your Angels

- Invite Your Angels to Join You
  - Silently or aloud, say:
    - "I call upon my angels, spirit guides, and higher self to show me angel numbers and to help me understand their messages. I am open, I am ready, I am listening."
  - Feel Their Presence

  - Take a few moments to feel the energy around you. You may notice a sensation of warmth, a gentle tingling, or a feeling of peace. Trust that your angels are present with you.

- Visualizing Angel Numbers - Imagine a Blank Screen or Chalkboard
  - In your mind's eye, visualize a blank screen or a chalkboard in front of you.

  - Ask your angels to reveal an angel number that you need to see right now. Say:
    - "Please show me a number sequence that holds a message for me."

  - Be Patient and Open

  - Relax and allow the numbers to appear. You might see them as if they're written on the screen, or they may pop into your mind as a sudden thought or image.

  - Don't force it. Simply observe whatever comes up, whether it's a single digit, a repeating sequence like 111 or 444, or a unique combination.

- Always thank your guides for sending you messages.

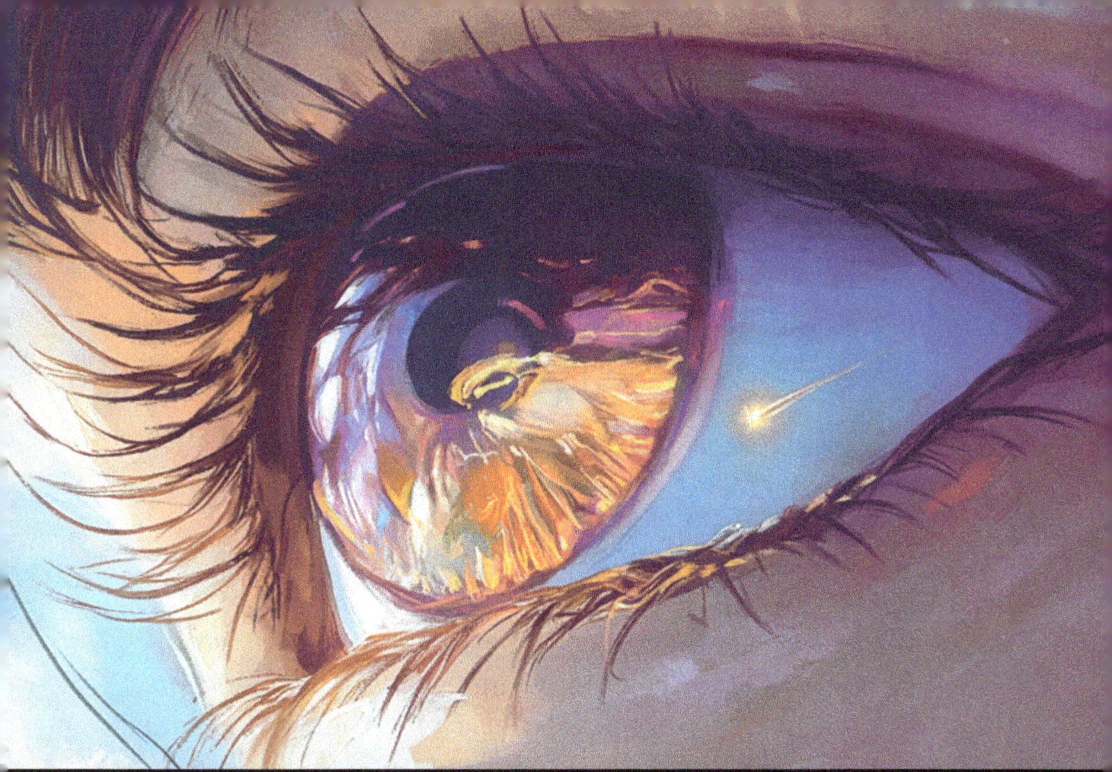

Intuitive Abilities - CLAIR'S

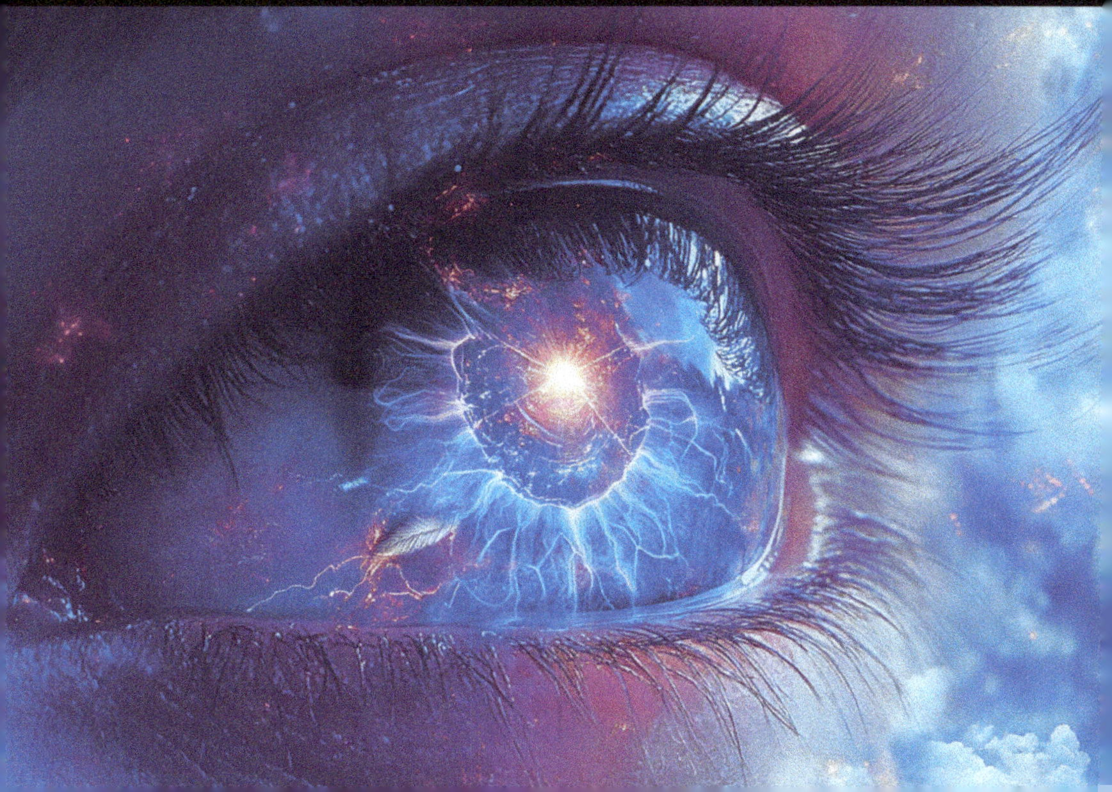

The "Clairs" refer to the various intuitive or psychic abilities that allow individuals to receive information beyond the physical senses.

- Each clair represents a different way of perceiving subtle energy, messages, or impressions from beyond the physical realm.
- These abilities are often linked to the third eye chakra and crown chakra, but they can also be connected to other chakras depending on the type of perception.

1. Clairvoyance (Clear Seeing)
- **What It Is:** The ability to see beyond the physical world. Clairvoyants receive intuitive information through mental images, visions, or symbols. This can include seeing auras, spirits, or glimpses of future events.
- **How It Manifests:** You might see images in your mind's eye, like a movie playing in your head. Sometimes, clairvoyance involves seeing flashes of light, colors, or symbolic imagery that has a deeper meaning.
- **Signs You Have It:** Vivid dreams, strong visualization skills, or frequently daydreaming in detailed imagery.

2. Clairaudience (Clear Hearing)
- **What It Is:** The ability to hear messages, sounds, or words that are not audible to the physical ear. This can include hearing guidance from spirit guides, angels, or deceased loved ones.
- **How It Manifests:** Clairaudient messages can come through as a voice in your mind, similar to how you "hear" your own thoughts. It may also involve hearing actual sounds, music, or even your name being called when no one is around.
- **Signs You Have It:** You might often hear ringing in your ears, receive sudden thoughts that feel like they're not your own, or be sensitive to sounds.

3. Clairsentience (Clear Feeling)
- **What It Is**: The ability to receive intuitive information through emotions and physical sensations. Clairsentients often sense the energy, emotions, or pain of other people, places, or situations.

- **How It Manifests:** This can include feeling someone else's emotions as if they were your own, getting a strong gut feeling, or experiencing physical sensations, like chills or warmth, when encountering certain people or places.

- **Signs You Have It:** Empaths often have clairsentience, feeling overwhelmed in crowded places or easily picking up on the emotions of others.

4. Claircognizance (Clear Knowing)
- **What It Is:** The ability to "just know" something without being able to explain how you know it. This knowledge often comes suddenly, like a burst of insight or a strong hunch.

- **How It Manifests:** You might receive information or answers to questions instantly, without any prior knowledge. This often feels like a download of information or a sudden "aha" moment.

- **Signs You Have It:** You tend to trust your gut instincts, frequently have accurate hunches, and often just "know" things without logical reasoning.

5. Clairgustance (Clear Tasting)
- **What It Is:** The ability to taste something without actually eating it. This is usually associated with tasting something that connects to a spirit or memory.

- **How It Manifests**: You might smell a specific perfume, flowers, smoke, or other scents that relate to a deceased loved one or a spirit trying to communicate.

- **Signs You Have It:** Suddenly smelling scents like roses, tobacco, or your grandmother's perfume without any physical source.

7. Clairtangency (Clear Touch) or Psychometry

- **What It Is:** The ability to receive information by touching an object or person. This often involves reading the energy or history of the object, place, or person.

- **How It Manifests:** By holding an object, you might receive impressions, images, or feelings about its past or the person it belonged to.

- **Signs You Have It:** Feeling drawn to touch items or experiencing sensations when you hold or touch something.

How to Develop Your "Clairs" - strengthen your intuitive abilities by doing the following:

- **Meditate Regularly:** Meditation helps clear your mind, enhance focus, and open your intuitive channels.

- **Keep a Journal:** Write down your intuitive impressions, dreams, or random thoughts that come to you. Over time, you may notice patterns.

- **Practice Visualization:** This helps enhance clairvoyance. Close your eyes and imagine detailed scenes, colors, or symbols.

- **Trust Your Gut Feelings:** Listen to your inner voice and act on your instincts to strengthen claircognizance and clairsentience.

- **Use Tools:** Crystals, tarot cards, or pendulums can help enhance your intuitive senses.

- **Ground Yourself:** Balancing your energy helps you stay clear and receptive. Try grounding exercises like walking barefoot on grass or working with grounding crystals like black tourmaline.

- **Most importantly:** your Chakras must be aligned and healthy to operate in your Clair's or higher gifts.

By exploring and practicing these abilities, you can better understand which "Clair" is strongest for you and how to develop your intuitive gifts.

- It is important to know that higher sensory perception or what some call SUPERPOWERS cannot activate until you unblock and balance your chakras.

- This is a daily process to keep your chakras balanced and can only be done by you.

- There are no shortcuts to unblocking and balancing your chakras. This is the first step to innerstand.

- As your chakras are cleared, your chakras will reveal the old programming you need to let go of.

- Your intuition and discernment will level up. This does not happen overnight so be kind to yourself.

- As you level up, your discernment will quickly reveal matrixes or DISTRACTIONS that were created for energy grabs. When those are revealed to you, you will have the choice to let them go.

- I call this acknowledge them and RELEASE THEM! DO NOT beat yourself up over it. You are growing and doing an amazing job.

By exploring and practicing these abilities, you can better understand which "Clair" is strongest for you and how to develop your intuitive gifts.

Soon you will notice your chakras changing, then you will know it is time to move into your morphogenetic chakras or HIGHER CHAKRAS. Congratulations!!

THE ASCENSION

To make this shift, we must adjust our mindset and actions to align with our soul's purpose and true essence. Key qualities like "Surrender" and "Acceptance" will help us through this process.

To let go of old behaviors and thought patterns that no longer serve us, we must first become aware of the beliefs and imbalances within us. Once we recognize them, we can take steps to clear or integrate them.

This journey will bring up deep fears, limiting beliefs, and past pains, triggered by events that make us aware of them. Some of these issues may stem from ancestral patterns, feeling both strange and familiar when they surface.

We are already coexisting in a strange world, but it's about to get weirder. Some of us may perceive this bifurcation (timeline) split happening more than others.

By focusing on higher knowledge of our Multidimensionality, we raise our energy to higher frequencies. This shift happens at levels of awareness beyond our conscious mind.

The path of conscious evolution, or Ascension, requires us to master our energy field so we can co-create with God. While we are creators, it's important to understand what this truly means. Instead of reacting impulsively from a victim mindset—since reacting brings out the Victim-Victimizer archetype and lowers our consciousness—we must shift our perspective.

When we feel powerless, we believe we have no control over our lives. To evolve, we need to clear our Negative Ego and stop getting stuck in painful thought patterns that keep us trapped in cycles of suffering.

As you continue on this journey of awakening, remember that the path to expanded consciousness is not a destination, but a continual unfolding. Every moment offers an opportunity to deepen your awareness, embrace your inner wisdom, and align with the infinite potential that resides within you.

Trust the process, honor your growth, and know that as you expand your consciousness, you contribute to the collective awakening of humanity.

The universe is waiting for you to step into your highest expression—now is the time to embrace it fully. Let your heart be your guide, and may your journey be filled with light, love, and boundless possibilities.

5D Navigator Journal
By Lisa Renee and Chris Mayer

- The **5D Navigator Journal** is a powerful tool for deepening your spiritual journey and expanding your consciousness. Created by spiritual teachers Lisa Renee and Chris Mayer, this interactive journal offers guided tools and practical insights to simplify and support your path of ascension, energy healing, and self-realization.
- Designed to help you integrate higher wisdom and navigate your personal growth, this journal provides space for reflection, meditation, and tracking your spiritual progress.
- Whether you're a beginner or an experienced seeker, it's the perfect companion to help you process energetic shifts and align with your true self.
- These are the same tools we use.

EXIT POINTS:

- Many people around us are currently choosing to exit this life. There seems to be a unique opening until the end of the year where individuals may decide whether to stay or leave the Earth plane.

- We are completing cycles, and for some, this means their contract is ending. You may witness loved ones facing illness, accidents, or sudden departures, which can be shocking and unexpected.

- It's important to stay in a peaceful, loving state of Engaged Neutrality, paired with deep compassion, as this is part of the process.

- Not everyone is here to experience physical ascension and may need to leave their body to evolve. Remember, as sovereign beings, everyone is following their path of evolution and moving to the station to evolve.

- Because you are here, reading this message - be assured, you are moving onto 5D.

- Many of us are being called to assist with these transitions, helping families and friends understand the process of passing over. If this is your role, thank you for your loving support—it is deeply needed at this time.

www.ingramcontent.com/pod-product-compliance
Lightning Source LLC
Chambersburg PA
CBHW051942160426
43198CB00013B/2267